What Every
Volunteer Youth Worker
Should Know

DANNY BRIERLEY

Authentic
LIFESTYLE

Copyright © 2003 Danny Brierley

First published in 2003 by Spring Harvest Publishing Division
and Authentic Lifestyle

11 10 09 08 07 06 05   8 7 6 5 4 3 2

Reprinted in 2005 by Authentic Media
9 Holdom Avenue, Bletchley, Milton Keynes, Bucks., MK1 1QR
and
29 Mobilization Drive, Waynesboro, GA 30830-4575, USA
www. authenticmedia.co.uk

British Library Cataloguing in Publication Data

A catalogue record for this book is available from the British Library

ISBN 1-85078-541-4

Print Management by Adare Carwin
Printed and Bound in Denmark by Nørhaven Paperback

Contents

Dedicated to Brenda and Tony Strickett, volunteer youth workers who invested considerable time and energy in me during my own teenage years.

Also by Danny Brierley

Young People and Small Groups

Joined Up: An Introduction to Youth Work and Ministry

Growing Community: Making Groups Work with Young People

Preface

What Every Volunteer Youth Worker Should Know has been written for busy 'extra-timers'. That's those who use their precious spare time to work voluntarily with young people. It doesn't claim to answer every question or meet every need. But it does provide a basic foundation in youth work and ministry that will equip you to do an even better job. I hope reading this will give you greater confidence and encouragement to continue serving the young people in your local community.

Every book is the result of a team effort and this is no exception. I am grateful to Mark Gadsden for his contribution towards the early thinking of the project and to Fiona Poulson, tutor on the Oasis Youth Work and Ministry Degree, for her assistance in developing some of the accompanying course materials into this book.

As part of Youthwork – the Partnership, I enjoy the support and encouragement of Richard Bromley (YfC), John Buckeridge (Youthwork Magazine), Jim Partridge (Spring Harvest), and Russell Rook (Salvation Army). This has become a creative and dynamic friendship. Steven May-Miller (Spring Harvest), Simon Warner (Spring Harvest), and Mark Finnie (Authentic) also deserve special mention.

I am also grateful to all the Oasis staff, associates, volunteers and students, for their dedication and passion for young people and youth workers. Without them, the church would be worse off.

Above all, I am thankful to all the hundreds of volunteer youth workers I have worked with over the years and, in particular, those at both Altrincham Baptist Church and Chawn Hill Christian Centre. I have received my reward in full, and paid the tax. They, on the other hand, must wait for their heavenly reward – but at least when it comes, it will be tax-free.

Danny Brierley, 2003

Introduction

This book is written for 'extra-timers' – those people who use their precious spare time to work voluntarily with young people. They don't get paid, are rarely thanked and yet without them society would be much the worse. Maybe you're one of them. If so, read on.

After years of decline, the church has emerged as the largest provider of youth work in the United Kingdom. There are an estimated 7,900 full-time, paid youth workers employed by churches in England and Wales alone.[1] Comparable research commissioned by the government-funded National Youth Agency found that all the local authorities in England and Wales accounted for just 3,190 full-time paid staff.[2] However, local authorities tend to rely on part-time paid staff and when these are factored in the end result is a respectable 7,190 full-time equivalent workers. However, this still leaves the Christian church as the largest employer of full-time paid youth workers in the country.

That's good news. But it gets better.

Whereas local authorities can muster hundreds of volunteers, the Christian church mobilises them by the tens of thousands. Almost two-thirds of the 50,000 churches in the UK[3] have at least one person who is actively involved with young people. Recent research by the Churches Information for Mission[4] found that in England alone there are at least 87,000 'extra-timers' who, week in week out, volunteer to serve the young. You are not alone.

These volunteers come from all walks of life and represent a diverse spread of ages and ethnicity. Any experienced full-time youth worker will freely admit that it is volunteers who make the real difference. That has certainly been the case in the churches I have served. I have only ever been as good as the volunteers who have worked with me.

Some people volunteer because they see the need and believe that they can make a real difference in young people's lives. Others get roped in by their friends, perhaps initially to help out with a one-off activity. That was three years ago and now they are roping in their friends – just to help out with a one-off activity you understand! Then there are those who put their hand up at the wrong moment in a church meeting. They thought were voting for a new heating system; in fact they were volunteering to run the youth group. Now, with no one else available, the young people plead with their puppy eyes not to abandon them.

Despite the importance of their task, many volunteers report feeling isolated and under-valued. Some struggle to know how best to serve young people, having few resources and even less training. Tragically, some eventually give up. Not only does this put even more pressure on the remaining volunteers but it also confuses young people. Faced with much uncertainty and turmoil in their lives, many young people come to rely on the support offered to them by youth workers. A high turnover of volunteers undermines the commitment of the church towards the young. This is not to emotionally blackmail you from ever resigning, but rather to challenge the church to offer you greater support and encouragement.

What Every Volunteer Youth Worker Should Know has been written for busy 'extra-timers' like you. It will provide you with a basic foundation in youth work and ministry and enable you to be an even better youth worker. It doesn't profess to offer answers to every question or be the last word on youth work. I hope you will gain greater confidence and encouragement to continue serving the young people in your local community.

What Every Volunteer Youth Worker Should Know is divided into four parts: understanding, working, developing and resourcing.

Part One opens in Chapter One with an introduction to youth work and ministry. It demonstrates how the five core values of voluntary participation, informal education, empowerment, equality of opportunity and incarnation are relevant to your group. This chapter will help you understand the purpose of, and approach to, youth work and ministry.

This is followed in Chapter Two by an introduction to adolescence. Hairy bits, dangly bits and wobbly bits all feature as we delve into the strange and confusing world of puberty, adolescence and the teenager. Young people are greatly influenced both by their physical development and their social environment. This chapter will enable you to better understand the young people you are working with.

Chapter Three provides a basic understanding of safe practice. Young people are too precious and the world too chaotic to tolerate irresponsible youth work and ministry. An awareness of risk assessment, child protection and appropriate methods of discipline are essential for today's volunteer youth workers. Ignorance is no excuse. This chapter will equip you with a basic understanding of good practice, and marks the end of Part One.

Part Two kicks off in Chapter Four with a look at working with individuals. Whilst many young people cope well with adolescence, some do not. For them, it is a struggle. Equally, it can be challenging for youth workers to know how best to establish a rapport with individuals. This chapter will help you to connect effectively with, and listen to, young people. It will also guide you through the moral maze of confidentiality and referral.

Working with groups is the focus of Chapter Five. Small groups or cells have become an established part of many youth projects or churches. Most groups comprise an assortment of characters, making the dynamics sometimes difficult to manage. Knowing what leadership style to adopt can sometimes be difficult. This chapter will equip you to be a more effective small or cell group leader.

In Chapter Six we take time out to look at ways of working more effectively. Life can be busy and youth work and ministry demanding. So much so, we sometimes neglect our own needs and risk losing our focus. This chapter will encourage you to value yourself, as well as the young people you serve, and marks the end of Part Two.

Part Three opens in Chapter Seven with a look at developing outreach. God's inclusive kingdom is truly good news for everyone, but especially for those who feel marginalised. And yet the church tends to focus its resources on serving its own members. Youth work and ministry, with its strong relational emphasis, adopts an holistic approach to reaching young people. This chapter will enable you to motivate your group members to reach their peers and, in so doing, to grow your youth work and ministry.

The spiritual journey continues in Chapter Eight with a look at developing spirituality. Young people are born with a God-given spiritual nature that finds ultimate satisfaction in Christ. Authentic Christian discipleship challenges today's 'entertain me' culture and calls on young people to pursue spiritual disciplines. A youth work and ministry approach to worship, Bible reading and giving are explored. This chapter will enable you to create a spiritually inspiring environment that enables young people to discover their God-given spiritual capacity and, ultimately, become more Christ-like.

Chapter Nine concludes Part Three with a look at developing programmes. Youth groups thrive on healthy, balanced programmes that meet young people's developmental needs. Likewise, youth groups are often only as good as their last session. Consequently, many youth workers struggle to come up with ideas week in, week out. This chapter will enable you to construct a healthy, balanced youth programme and plan creative and challenging sessions.

Finally, on the basis that youth workers are only as good as the last ideas they begged, borrowed or stole, Part Four contains 70 'tried and tested' ideas for you to use in your youth work and ministry. There is also a Resource Directory listing useful organisations, resources and sources of further information.

This truly is what every volunteer youth worker should know. We begin with an understanding of youth work and ministry.

NOTES

1 Brierley, P. (2000), *The Tide is Running Out: What the English Church Attendance Survey Reveals*, London: Christian Research.
2 Marken, M. et al (1998), *England's Youth Service – the 1998 Audit*, Leicester: Youth Work Press.
3 Brierley, P. & Wraight, H. (2001), *Religious Trends 3*, London: Christian Research.
4 Geldor, A. & Escott, P. (2003), *Profile of Youth Workers*, London: Churches Information for Mission.

What Every Volunteer Youth Worker Should Know – the Course

Whilst there is much to gain from reading *What Every Volunteer Youth Worker Should Know* on your own, you will derive maximum benefit from completing the accompanying course.

The flexible course comprises nine two-hour sessions and can be completed one evening a week over a term, one evening a month during a year or in three full days. These creative and interactive sessions provide an opportunity to discuss with fellow extra-timers and the course trainer what every volunteer youth worker should know. Also included are more tried and tested ideas for you to use with your group.

What Every Volunteer Youth Worker Should Know – the Course is designed and delivered by Oasis Youth Action, with support from the Salvation Army, and forms part of Youthwork – the Training. For further information, please visit www.oasistrust.org/youthvolunteerscourse/ or call 020 7450 9044.

Part One

UNDERSTANDING

1

Understanding youth work and ministry

My name is Danny Brierley and I am – err – an activist. I thought I could handle it. I'd see a task and just start doing something, anything; it didn't matter what. After all, those that can, do; those that can't, just reflect. Right? But after a while it started to affect others.

On one occasion I remember, I was taking a group of young people on an all-night walk through a forest in Wales. We were on an adventure and, being Mr Activist, I was in heaven. Only I hadn't given the young people any safety instructions, or told them where we were heading. As the minibus rolled to a stop in the Forestry Commission car park, all the young people leapt out and scattered into the forest. It was pitch black and I had lost twelve young people in a forest within thirty seconds of arriving. I couldn't stop them, could I? I was behind the wheel. Someone had to drive the minibus. I couldn't believe what I'd done. How was I going to tell their parents? The drive home was going to be eerily quiet. If only I'd stopped to think about what I was doing and where we were going? This was when I first realised my activism had got hold of me.

To my shame, this incident actually happened. The forest was near Symonds Yat and the year was 1992.

Fortunately, no one was permanently lost that night, but I learnt a valuable lesson. Thinking ahead is an essential part of any youth work.

Serving as an 'extra timer', no matter how you came to be involved, means you now have responsibilities towards the young people in your group. But what are you meant to be doing? Come to think of it, what actually is youth work and ministry? This chapter looks at God's passion for young people and what they can teach us. But it also explores the basis for, and values of, youth work and ministry.

Why work with young people?

Working with young people is normally very satisfying. Many youth workers enjoy their sense of fun and irreverence; others, their enthusiasm and energy. Being with young people who are experiencing crisis can also be a privilege and it is often humbling to see the change they bring about. Yet there are times when youth work and ministry is also quite challenging. Even the most dedicated youth worker has the occasional 'off' day.

Imagine that it's Youth Night. After a demanding day at work – in your home or outside it – you arrive at the youth group location and spend thirty frantic minutes preparing for the young people's arrival. For the next two hours you multitask: chatting to young people, organising activities, keeping an eye out for new members and discreetly monitoring the venue. Afterwards, you spend twenty minutes tidying away equipment, re-filling emptied fire extinguishers and carrying out minor repairs to the building – enough at least to implicate the senior citizens who also used the building that day. Though exhausted by the time you get home, you are nevertheless satisfied with the meaningful conversations you have had with young people. After thirty minutes of television you begin to feel human again.

On Sunday morning, expecting at least a little appreciation for all you have done, you are greeted at church with a list of complaints about the state of the hall. The senior citizens had an alibi. No one asks about the young people in your group. Sometimes it is easy to feel discouraged and forget why we work with young people. So why do we do it?

To think about...
Why do you work with young people? What motivates you?

There are two broad reasons why so many Christians work with young people. First, God is passionate about the young; and second, they make great teachers. Let me explain.

God is passionate about young people

If God is passionate about young people then it makes sense for us share in this passion also. But what is the basis for this?

1. *God values young people*

Like adults and children, they are all made in his image (Gen. 1:27). Paul describes people as being God's work of art (Eph. 2:10). Literally, everyone – young people included – is one of God's masterpieces, a priceless art treasure. Tragically, too many young people feel worthless and 'trashed' as a result of negative life experiences. Youth work and ministry demonstrates to them their inherent worth and offers them an opportunity to experience God's love – as conducted through your life and witness. Young people are not a 'problem' to be solved; they are VIPs to be served.

2. *God understands young people*

As well as being passionate about them, God completely understands them. Strange as it may sound, he was once a teenager. God the Son was born as a baby and grew into an adult. Biologically, there is no way to achieve this without passing through adolescence – even for God the Son. Jesus' parents did not always understand him (Lk. 2:48). Despite this, Luke tells us that 'Jesus grew in wisdom and stature, and in favour with God and men' (Lk. 2:52). God understands what it is to be young; he has first-hand experience of adolescence.

3. *God empowers young people*

The Bible is full of young people God has empowered to do remarkable things. For example, Joseph was a young man with an outlandish sense of fashion who went on to achieve high office and rescue his fellow people. Moses was a hot-tempered young man who went on to lead the Israelites from captivity into freedom. Mary was a teenager in love who found herself pregnant by the Holy Spirit. She gave birth to Jesus, God the Son. Today, God continues to enable young people to do great things for him.

Young people make great teachers

I believe the second reason why we work with young people is because of what they can teach us. Whatever we give to them, they offer back twice over.

1. *Young people deepen our faith and witness*
   They help us to 'keep it real'. Young people are rarely prepared to accept glib answers to complex questions. They challenge our pompous attitudes and religiosity, and are quick to point out inconsistencies between what we say and do. Young people often bring fresh understanding to our faith and witness. For example, they remind us that belonging is more important than attending and that worship is a matter of the heart as well as the head.

2. *Young people prepare us for the future*
   They often bring about change by challenging the status quo. Today's radical youth subculture often becomes tomorrow's mainstream culture. Working with young people gives us a glimpse of the future and therefore enables us to prepare future strategies. Andy Hickford powerfully articulates this in his book, *Essential Youth*.[1] But young people are not just the church of tomorrow, they are the church of today.

If God is passionate about young people and we can learn so much from them, then there can be no excuse for thoughtless youth work and ministry. It is far too important to be simply thrown together.

What is youth work and ministry?

So what exactly is youth work and ministry? This is not such a foolish question as it may at first appear. Not everyone who works with the young is a youth worker and not everything involving young people is youth work. For example, police officers may work with the young – arresting them if they break the law – but this is not youth work *per se*. Likewise, teachers work with the young to educate them, but this is different from youth work. Playing pool at a youth club with a young person is not necessarily youth work if its focus is providing an entertaining activity.

For an activity to be considered youth work it must be both educative and voluntary. Though the activities may be informal, there must be an intention to foster young people's development. The young people must participate because they choose to, not because they are forced to.

Some people engage in youth work, defined as emphasising the personal and social development of young people without reference to spirituality. Others engage in youth ministry, defined as emphasising the spiritual development of young people without ever referring to their personal and social development. Put the two together and you get youth work and ministry. It is both/and, not either/or. I wrote about this in greater depth in *Joined Up: An Introduction to Youth Work and Ministry*.[2]

Youth work and ministry facilitates a young person's personal, social, spiritual and educational development. It enables them to achieve their God-given potential, and have a voice, influence and role in their community (including church, school, family and neighbourhood), during their transition from dependence to inter-dependence. Youth work and ministry is shaped by five core values:

● Voluntary participation
● Informal education
● Empowerment
● Equality of opportunity
● Incarnation

Values of youth work and ministry

Voluntary participation

Some young people are forced to attend church youth activities by their Christian parents. Though prompted by good intentions, involuntary participation can be counter-productive. Young people who attend youth activities under duress often register their protest by disengaging from the programme and/or taking it out on the youth workers. It can be a no-win situation for the young people, their parents and the youth workers. Youth work and ministry is based on a voluntary relationship between young people and youth workers. It cannot involve compulsory attendance. This is why police work is not youth work. Young people must participate because they want to, not because they are forced to.

Voluntary participation also calls for young people to be active partners in the learning process and decision-making structures. They should be participants in, not just consumers of, the youth programme.

Jesus modelled voluntary participation. He invited, never forced, people to follow him (Mt. 4:18–22; Lk. 5:1–11,27–32). He respected each person's right to choose (Lk. 9:51–56). He accepted that not every invitation would be taken up (Mt. 8:18–22; 19:16–22). He included both the 'sure' and 'unsure' (Mt. 16:13–19; Jn. 12:4; 14:5; 20:24–28) and enabled those who opted in to make significant contributions (Lk. 6:12–16; 9:1–6,28–36; 10:1–12).

Youth work and ministry provides young people with a safe place in which to explore issues, beliefs and skills. We must respect their right to choose whether they participate in the activities we provide. This means risking the possibility that they may prefer to do something else with their time and energy. But this is precisely the risk that God takes with us.

To think about...
To what extent do the young people you serve participate because they want to? What difference does, or would, voluntary participation make to your youth work and ministry?

Informal education

Secondary schools use a formal approach to instructing pupils. Those in authority set the agenda and determine what is taught. This is perfectly valid, but it isn't youth work and ministry. Some church youth programmes make effective use of creative teaching aids, such as videos and games, within the formal model. For example, the youth workers – not the young people – do most of the talking and decision-making.

Unlike formal education, youth work and ministry is responsive to the diverse interests and needs of young people. It is based on informal education. It starts where they are at, not where the curriculum says they should be. Youth work and ministry creates, and makes use of, opportunities to develop the skills, attitudes and beliefs of the young people. As well as using fun and culturally relevant methods, youth work and ministry fosters learning through conversations, group work and activities. Learning and change can be brought about through planned activities (e.g. a group session on friendship), but can equally result from opportunities that arise spontaneously (e.g. a conversation about friendship). Informal education is more than a few games and a fistful of video clips interspersed with teaching points all beginning with 'P'.

Jesus modelled informal education. He rarely used formal settings or specific communication methods. He engaged in conversation to bring about learning (Lk. 11:1–13; Jn. 4:4–26). He told stories and parables that enabled people to think for themselves (Mt. 7:24–29; Lk. 8:9–10) and talked in pictures and symbols (Jn. 6:35; 8:12; 10:7; 10:11; 11:25; 14:6; 15:1). He performed miracles to demonstrate and explain the reality of the kingdom (Mt. 9:1–8). And he taught people by his example; his life and actions spoke volumes (Mk. 1:21–22).

Imagine some young people ask you to explain why the four Gospels appear to be so different when they are supposedly written about the same basic events. You could respond with a technically correct, if complex and dull, answer about hermeneutics and literary criticism. Alternatively, you could do what I once did with a group who asked me this question. Without warning, I ran and skipped around the room, singing "I'm forever blowing bubbles" at the top of my voice, before ending with some rather athletic press ups and star jumps. I then sat down to stunned silence from the young people, and when I'd got my breath back I asked them to write down what they had just witnessed. Despite having all observed the same event, each came up with a slightly different version. Some focused on chronology, recording that I began by skipping. Others concentrated on interpretation, suggesting cruelly that I had gone mad.

In just the same way, the four gospel writers wrote about the same events from their own perspectives. Matthew, who was writing to a Jewish audience, highlighted Jesus' Jewish credentials. Mark, who wrote his gospel first, gave the shortest account, and focused on the practical side to Jesus' life. Luke wrote for a Gentile audience, and so highlighted Jesus' inclusive nature. John, who wrote last and more visually, was more interested in interpretation than factual events.

In the same way today, journalists tailor their reporting of events for different audiences. Take, for example, a fire on a North Sea oil rig. *The Times* might report on the facts and figures of casualties and environmental damage, while the *Financial Times* might lead on the insurance market implications. *The Sun* may perhaps opt for the one-word headline 'Hero' and a story about the heroism of an individual, with a stunning photograph of the burning rig. This just leaves the *Daily Star* to report that yet another Volkswagen Beetle has been found on Mars – clamped.

You could, of course, plan to teach all this as part of the curriculum, albeit in a lively and informative way. This would draw from formal education. However, by either making the most of the opportunity created by the question or by planning to use an attention grabbing challenge to raise the issue, you could actively involve the young people in the learning process. This is informal education.

To think about...
What opportunities do you have for informal education in your youth work and ministry? When have you been able to use informal education methods to good effect? How confident would you feel about informal education?

Empowerment

Some church youth groups simply expect young people to attend, consuming whatever the youth worker offers. This may empower the youth worker, but it will disempower the young people. Thankfully, others view young people as full participants. Although we live in a consumer society, youth work and ministry must be more than a commodity if it is to empower young people to reach their full God-given potential.

Youth work and ministry supports young people in their quest for responsibility. It enables them to take greater ownership of their lives and the communities of which they are a part. Society is inherently unjust, with power often used by the few to limit the opportunities of the many. Even in a democracy, not all voices are listened to. Given the right conditions, though, young people empower themselves. Some people have the ability to make us feel better about ourselves and our abilities. That's the kind of environment we need to create for the young people we serve.

Jesus modelled empowerment. He affirmed people regardless of their status (Mt. 5:3–12; 6:25–34). He demonstrated the power of prayer for all people (Mt. 7:7–8). He made God's Holy Spirit available to all (Jn. 14:15–21; 16:5–16). He commissioned ordinary people to do great works (Mt. 28:18–20; Lk. 10:1–3). He anointed people to perform signs and wonders (Mt. 10:1; Lk. 10:8–12; Jn. 14:12–14). And he enabled the church to take over his work once he had ascended (Acts 1).

The challenge is for us to create this same positive attitude towards young people; one that enables them to achieve considerably more than they ever thought possible. This is not the same as unrealistic flattery, which can be destructive.

To think about...
To what extent are young people able to affect decisions in your youth project and/or church? What difference does this make?

Equality of opportunity

Many young people are denied the benefits of society. Many face discrimination on the basis of gender, ethnicity, culture, sexual orientation, skin colour, age, wealth and so forth. Youth work and ministry celebrates diversity and challenges discrimination, seeking equality of opportunity. Youth work and ministry helps young people to identify and challenge oppressions such as racism and sexism, and all other -isms that spring from differences of culture, ethnicity, language, gender, ability, age, religion and class.

Jesus modelled equality of opportunity. His actions challenged discrimination against young people and children (Mt. 21:15–16; Lk. 18:15–17). He challenged discrimination against women (Mt. 9:18–25; Lk. 10:38–42), the poor (Mk. 12:41–44), disabled people (Mt. 9:1–8,27–32), those infected by illness and disease (Mt. 8:1–4), and against those regarded as 'sinners' (Mt. 9:9–13). He was inclusive of all – even people like me.

The question is, in our youth work and ministry do we model the same inclusion of all? What groups of young people do we – intentionally or unintentionally – exclude? What about the physical access to your buildings? These are important questions. Equality of opportunity is not simply political correctness; it is a matter of justice, enabling all those made in God's image to enjoy the full benefits that are available to the majority.

To think about...
How are you modelling equality of opportunity in your youth work and ministry? To what extent are you required to challenge oppressive language or behaviour? How have you done this?

Incarnation

The previous four values are common to youth work (secular) and youth ministry (sacred). However, youth work and ministry is holistic in its approach and adds a fifth value: incarnation. This means the 'embodiment of flesh' and is exactly what happened when God entered the world in the person of Jesus. Eugene H. Peterson, in *The Message*,[3] vividly translates the opening chapter of John's Gospel as:

The Word was first,
the Word present to God,
God present to the Word.
The Word was God,
in readiness for God from day one.

Everything was created through him;
nothing – not one thing! –
came into being without him.
What came into existence was Life,
and the Life was Light to live by.
The Life-Light blazed out of the darkness;
the darkness couldn't put it out.

There was once a man, his name John, sent by God to point out the way to the Life-Light. He came to show everyone where to look, who to believe in. John was not himself the Light; he was there to show the way to the Light.

The Life-Light was the real thing:
Every person entering Life
he brings into Light.
He was in the world,
the world was there through him,
and yet the world didn't even notice.
He came to his own people,
but they didn't want him.
But whoever did want him,
who believed he was who he claimed
and would do what he said,
He made to be their true selves,
their child-of-God selves.
These are the God-begotten,
not blood-begotten,
not flesh-begotten,
not sex-begotten.
The Word became flesh and blood,
and moved into the neighbourhood.
We saw the glory with our own eyes,
the one-of-a-kind glory,
like Father, like Son,
Generous inside and out,
true from start to finish.

John 1:1–14, *The Message*

The incarnation of Christ provides us with a model to emulate in our youth work and ministry. Just as Christ left the security and peace of heaven to 'move into your neighbourhood', so we are called to leave relative security and peace to enter the neighbourhood of young people. The incarnation reminds us to take the initiative in reaching out to young people. Youth work and ministry is mission. The four other values prevent our mission degenerating into indoctrination or cult-like practice. Youth work and ministry is profoundly spiritual; it enables young people to recognise and receive the 'Word made flesh and blood'. And all this is channelled through us.

To think about...
To what extent do you model the incarnate Christ in your youth work and ministry by leaving the relative security of your own surroundings in order to be among young people in their communities?

The five values of voluntary participation, informal education, empowerment, equality of opportunity and incarnation provide us with a framework for youth work and ministry that is both biblical and effective. The next chapter, 'Understanding young people', looks at puberty, adolescence and youth subcultures. Knowing more about young people – their experiences and the world they inhabit – enables us to forge stronger relationships with them.

Summary

- God is passionate about young people; he values and understands them.
- You can learn as much from young people as they can from you.

- Youth work and ministry is shaped by the five core values of voluntary participation, informal education, empowerment, equality of opportunity, and incarnation.
- Each of these values is modelled to us in the life and ministry of Jesus.

Notes

1. Hickford, A. (2003), *Essential Youth*, Carlisle: Authentic
2. Brierley, D. (2003), *Joined Up: An Introduction to Youth Work and Ministry*, Carlisle: Authentic
3. Peterson, E. (1993), *The Message*, Colorado Springs, USA: NavPress

2

Understanding young people

When working for churches, I have generally taken Tuesdays off. This has been my time to relax and unwind from some of the stresses of full-time youth work and ministry. It was on such a Tuesday that I spotted a group of familiar faces loitering outside The Vine. There were at least a dozen of them, and they were standing on my side of the road. Even from a distance, I recognised them immediately. My professional instincts told me to get prepared for another lively encounter, but my private emotions pleaded that it was a Tuesday and they were not my responsibility – at least not today. So, like the priest and the Levite in the Parable of the Good Samaritan, I crossed over to the other side. Perhaps they wouldn't recognise me.

As I got nearer, I could see that they were all dressed in the same style of clothes. They wore the uniform of belonging with pride. It made a statement about who they were and what they stood for. Most also had dyed hair. Closer still and I could see that some were even carrying sticks. By the time I was almost opposite them I could hear their distinctive language and familiar way of speaking. It was unmistakable. Why was this happening to me – on a Tuesday? It was no use; I had to engage. I was powerless to stop myself. What could possibly go wrong? After all, despite their numbers, group fashion statement, dyed hair, language and sticks, what harm could a gang of senior citizens do me? Yes, they were all well above retirement age and waiting outside the pub for the Community Transport bus to take them to bingo.

Young people receive much attention today, most of it negative. The media sensationalises stories of crime and delinquency to the point that peaceful, law-abiding young people are viewed with suspicion. For example, those most likely to be victims of crime in Britain are not the elderly or housebound but the young. It is true that a tiny minority of young people are responsible for a disproportionate level of crime. But it is not fair to stereotype all young people as criminals. This is rarely mentioned in reports about rises in 'youth crime'.

Those involved in youth work and ministry need to have a much better understanding of young people so that they can challenge popular misconceptions as they arise. This chapter starts with a look at the physical effects of adolescence brought about by puberty. Whilst many cope well with these changes, some are left emotionally scarred. Appreciating the dramatic effects of puberty will enable you to be more sensitive to the young people you serve. The chapter then moves on to look at culture and youth subcultures. Understanding this will enable you to better engage with those who inhabit a different cultural world.

Adolescent development

Youth work and ministry starts with understanding ourselves and how we relate to young people. We have all been shaped by different experiences, events and influences collected through life; these make us the people we are. Experiences gained during adolescence are, for most people, some of their most formative. Being aware of your own teenage experiences will enable you to better understand and value the young people you serve today.

To think about...

Think back to a different era, such as the sixties, seventies or eighties. What were young people wearing and listening to? What were some of the significant national and international events? What were some of the major issues that young people faced? Then compare this with your own experiences of youth. What are the similarities and differences?

Although perhaps obvious, it is worth stating at the outset that no two young people are the same. Every one is a unique individual, created and valued by God. The purpose here is not to generalise the normal adolescent experience, but to help you understand the effects and implications of this development on each individual you serve.

Youth is a stage of life

Christians approach human development from the premise that all people – young and old – are made in the image of God (Gen. 1:27). As such, they have inherent value and spiritual capacity. God created the natural order to facilitate the development of his creation. Built into creation is the natural process of reproduction, growth and development. Human development is characterised by a series of distinct and sequential stages that people gradually progress through. This lifelong journey begins with birth and, it is hoped, progresses through childhood into adulthood before concluding, in old age, with death. There is a logical sequence to these stages (e.g. childhood must come before adulthood) but no guarantee that everyone will complete all stages. We feel cheated when lives are 'cut short'.

Adolescence is a significant developmental stage.[1] It literally means to 'grow up' and marks the transition from childhood to adulthood. It is sometimes known as the flapping stage. Just as young birds learn to flap their wings and eventually fly off, so young people learn to leave behind the dependency of childhood and adopt more independent approaches to life that are normally associated with adulthood. Adolescence is characterised by significant physiological (physical), social, emotional and spiritual change. This is brought about by the onset of puberty.

Understanding physical development

During adolescence significant physical changes take place in the human body. This process is caused by puberty. For females, puberty normally begins with the onset of menstruation (periods) and for males with the development of pubic hair. However these are only part of a complex picture. Hormones released by the pituitary gland stimulate puberty. These hormones have a stimulating effect on the endocrine gland, which in turn releases growth related hormones. This process is also responsible for releasing sex hormones – testosterone in males and oestrogen in females. Therefore, a young person's sex drive is kicked off by the onset of the growth spurt.

There are five basic physiological changes that take place during puberty. These are:

1. Rapid acceleration in growth, commonly referred to as the growth spurt, that affects both height and weight.
2. Further development of the reproductive systems, these being the testes in males and the ovaries in females.
3. Development of secondary sex characteristics resulting in the emergence of pubic, facial and body hair and the further development of the sex organs. For males, this is the lengthening of the penis and, for females, the growth of breasts and the rounding of hips.
4. Changes in body composition, specifically in the quantity and distribution of fat and muscle.
5. Changes in the circulatory and respiratory systems that, in turn, lead to increased stamina and strength. The heart nearly doubles in weight and the lungs significantly expand. Males experience development of the larynx (Adam's apple), prompting the voice to 'break'.

In becoming incarnate, God the Son experienced life as a young person (Lk. 2:42). He experienced growth and maturation. If spots are a natural consequence of puberty then the teenage Son of God most certainly had them. Whether his prayers for them to go were answered faster than those of today's desperate young people – or if, being perfectly secure in his identity, he was unaffected by them – we must leave to theologians with excessive time on their hands. For now, it is sufficient to know that Christ experienced life as a teenager.

The psychological effects of puberty

Popular assertions that all young people experience 'storm and stress'[2] are exaggerated. Many young people cope well with adolescence and puberty. That said, significant changes to the body do have a profound psychological effect on some young people. Rapid increases in height and weight can result in clumsiness and self-consciousness. New body functions, such as periods for females or wet dreams for boys, can result in anxiety. Ignorance, fear, embarrassment and social taboo heighten some young people's self-consciousness and confusion.

Many young people have a false perception of what a normal body looks like and by when. Peers and the media contribute significantly to creating an image to which few young people can measure up. For many, this results in feelings of inadequacy. As a generalisation, boys tend to be concerned with their height whereas girls worry over their weight.

The timing of these physiological changes may also have a significant impact. Boys who experience puberty early are more likely to have a positive self-image, whereas late developers are more likely to have a negative attitude. In contrast, girls who reach puberty early are more likely to experience feelings of depression and anxiety and are generally less satisfied with their weight and appearance than are late developers.

A volunteer youth worker needs to know how young people may react to these changes, both in our one-to-one work and in the development of a youth programme. For example, sports-related activities can exaggerate differences in physical appearance and performance. Team efforts are less threatening than solo performances. Swimming can be unhelpful for many young people, especially girls. Also, young males are twice as likely to experience enuresis (bed-wetting) than are females. This has implications for residential activities.

To think about...
Knowing more about puberty, what changes, if any, do you need to make to the way you respond to young people in your group or to the content of your youth programme?

Youth subcultures

People are shaped by the culture they grow up in. The world is remarkably different in the 21st century from how it was when we were born. Technological advances (e.g. internet, mobile phones), globalization (world trade, international travel, brand awareness), the decline of religious institutions, and the fragmentation of community are just some of the influences forming today's young people.

Youth is starting earlier and ending later. Improvements in health mean that puberty is gradually beginning earlier for each successive generation. Likewise, media exposure ensures that children are now aware of matters previously reserved for older teenagers or adults. At the other end, the responsibilities of adulthood are being delayed through the extension of education. There was a time when many left formal education aged fourteen. This was extended to fifteen and then sixteen. Now, the British government plans for 50 per cent of young people to continue in full-time education until they are twenty-one. As a consequence, youth takes much longer to complete these days and with it the drive for independence. They are physically mature but society says they must wait before having adult privileges and responsibilities.

Culture and subcultures

Culture describes the way of life adopted by a majority group of people who share a common identity. It is the collection of ideas, language, fashion, rules and conventions that members are expected – implicitly or explicitly – to follow. Culture is learnt and passed on to successive generations through a process of rewards and punishments. This process is called socialisation. It is the majority culture that determines what is 'normal'.

A subculture is formed when a minority group begins to identify itself as being different from the majority. Common values, words, fashions, rules and conventions bind together members of the group, providing an alternative belonging and identity. It is better to think of there being a series of youth subcultures, rather than one unified youth culture. Some youth subcultures are based around a shared fashion or activity (such as skateboarding or surfing) and have national or international appeal. Others are localized.

To think about...
What subcultures exist in your community and youth work and ministry, and what symbols (e.g. fashion, music, language etc.) help to identify them?

Understanding youth subcultures

Youth subcultures are radical. They challenge 'norms'. Mainstream culture always feels threatened by subcultures, which are seen as destabilising and a danger to its existence. To protect itself and preserve the status quo, the conservative mainstream must either fight off or tame all subversive subcultures. In reality, however, the future well-being of society often rests with the few minority subcultures that are capable of challenging the majority. We need 'rebellious' young people to challenge the status quo if we are to cope with the wider problems and challenges of society.

A successful subculture becomes the mainstream. What began as a radical and subversive minority often gains gradual acceptance as the 'norm' by the majority. This is particularly evident with fashion and music. The radical youth subcultures of the 1960s have contributed their guitar-based folk music and informality in the choruses so well established in today's church.

The church desperately needs young people, but not just to fill seats in services. We need them to challenge our traditions, culture and theology. Only then can tomorrow's church be relevant. The process of change can be as uncomfortable for the young people as it is for the church leaders and members. Part of your role is to enable the young people you serve to challenge the status quo in your congregation. Just remember that twenty years from now today's cultural revolutionaries will have become the mainstream, and the process of cultural evolution will continue with a new subculture.

To think about...
Identify a range of social influences that affect the young people you serve. What positive contribution can or do these make to the adult 'mainstream' culture of your church?

Young people under pressure

Young people have always been subject to exploitation. During the Industrial Revolution, young people were exploited in factories – working long hours for little financial reward. Now we are living through the media revolution, and young people are being exploited as consumers. The term 'teenager' was coined in the 1950s by the advertising industry, which was keen to create markets for the products being pumped out by factories no longer sustained by the war effort. In the new world economy, young people were a market to be exploited. Relentless and increasingly sophisticated advertising continues to rob young people of their individuality. Like all of us, young people become what they consume. Buying the latest shoe is not so much making a luxury purchase as staking an essential claim to belonging and self-identity.

Sometimes capitalist society borrows from the radical youth subculture for commercial advantage. For example, advertisers may use graffiti art to appeal to mainstream consumers who want something different. Young people are surrounded by social influences, some positive and others negative. It's not essential for youth workers and ministers to identify these influences. Effective youth work and ministry will enable the young people to identify them and choose which to embrace and which to reject.

Cultural relevance

The message of Jesus is relevant to all people, at all times and in all cultures. It is timeless truth. However, the way this truth is presented or modelled requires significant cultural adaptation. Missionaries have learnt the hard way that they need to respect, and allow for, different cultural perspectives when presenting Christianity. In the same way, Christian youth workers are missionaries to youth subcultures and must tailor their approach accordingly.

Matthew, Mark, Luke and John each wrote their gospel for a different audience, and tailored their approach accordingly. Matthew wrote for a Jewish audience (emphasising the Christ, fulfilment of Old Testament prophecies), whereas Luke wrote for the Gentiles (emphasising the role of women, children, the outcast). Jesus habitually used familiar metaphors that his audience could easily relate to. Paul made use of contemporary culture and the arts to communicate his message.

The attitude and approach of youth workers can make all the difference between acceptance and rejection of the Christian faith by a youth subculture. Using familiar language, activities and music, we can enable young people to respond more positively to our message. For the sake of young people and mission, it is sometimes necessary to change our church structures and traditions in order that some might believe.

To think about...
What do you believe needs to change if you and your practice are to be more effective in relating to youth subcultures? Can you think of examples of culturally relevant youth work and ministry?

Cultural irrelevance

It is sometimes appropriate to be counter-cultural, challenging the more destructive aspects of popular culture. When doing this we should be motivated by love and

speak with humility, but never adopt a judgmental attitude. Youth work and ministry seeks to provide young
people with safe opportunities to explore relevant issues.
This enables young people to identify and challenge
destructive aspects of popular culture for themselves.
This is far more effective than attempting to tell young
people what is good or bad for them.

The challenge is always to maintain tension between
cultural relevance and irrelevance. Too little relevance
and we fail to engage with youth subcultures beyond
the church; too little irrelevance and we fail to model
authentic Christianity to those who need it most.

In the next chapter, 'Understanding safe practice', we
shall look at child protection, health and safety, and
managing behaviour. These are essential to ensure the
safety and well-being of the young people we serve.

Summary

- No two young people are the same; they are all unique
  individuals. Equally, your experiences of youth were
  also unique and therefore different in many ways to
  those of today's young people.
- Youth work and ministry starts with understanding
  yourself and how you relate to the young people you
  serve.
- Adolescence is a stage of life brought about by the
  onset of puberty. Although most young people cope
  well with the effects of puberty, some experience emotional stress.
- Culture is the way of life adopted by a majority group
  of people who share a common identity. It is the collection of ideas, language, fashion, rules and conventions

that members are expected – implicitly or explicitly – to follow.

- Youth subcultures are radical, and often bring about change in mainstream society. The church needs young people because they challenge its traditions, culture and theology.
- Youth work and ministry looks for culturally relevant ways to engage with subcultures of young people.
- Youth work and ministry will also sometimes need to be culturally irrelevant, challenging negative aspects of youth subcultures.

NOTES

1. For a more in-depth review of adolescence, please see John Coleman & Leo Hendry's *The Nature of Adolescence* (Routledge, 1999)
2. G. Stanley Hall, credited as being the father of psychology, established the first psychology lab in 1883.

3

Understanding safe practice

Dear Mum and Dad

We're having a great time here at Lake Typhoid. Scoutmaster Webb is making us all write to our parents in case you saw the flood on TV and were worried. We are OK. Only one of our tents and two sleeping bags got washed away. Luckily none of us drowned because we were on the mountain looking for Sam when it happened.

Oh yes, please call Sam's mother and tell her he's OK. He can't write because of the cast. I got to ride in a search and rescue Land Rover. It was fun. We never would have found him in the dark if not for the lightning. Scoutmaster Webb got mad at Sam for going on a hike alone without telling anyone. Sam said he did tell him, but it was during the fire, so he probably didn't hear him.

Did you know that if you put petrol on a fire, the petrol can will blow up? The wet wood still didn't burn, but one of our tents did. Also some of our clothes. John will look weird until his hair grows back.

Guess what? We have all passed our first aid badges. When Dave dived into the lake and cut his arm, we got to see how a tourniquet works.

Also, James and I threw up. Scoutmaster Webb said it probably was just food poisoning from the leftover chicken. I have to go now. We're going into town to mail our letters and buy bullets. Don't worry about anything. We are fine; we're with Scoutmaster Webb.

Love Jack

PS. How long has it been since I had a tetanus shot?

This global email appeared in *The Times Magazine*.[1] I am sure none of the young people you serve would ever have cause to write such a letter. It is extreme and witty. But it also serves as a poignant reminder that you have a duty of care towards the young people you serve. This chapter looks at ways to create a safer environment.

Voluntary but not unprofessional

Most youth work and ministry is undertaken by volunteers (extra-timers), not paid staff (full-timers). Being volunteer-led does not mean it need – or should – be unprofessional. There was a time when voluntary youth work was thought to be above and beyond regulation. 'After all, they're only amateurs,' was the attitude. Anyone could set themself up as a youth worker and do almost anything with young people. When things went wrong, it was dismissed as 'character building'. Those who look back nostalgically often forget the harm done to some young people as a consequence.

To think about...
Is there anything you remember youth workers doing years ago that you now consider unacceptable?

Unprofessional youth work and ministry damages the reputation of the church. As a society, we no longer accept a cavalier approach to work with the young. Our 'blame culture' sadly causes some people to shy away from accepting responsibility for their actions. On a more positive note, however, we now have a higher regard for young people and look for ways to protect them from harm. Christians also desire to reflect God's heart towards his creation. In the Bible, shepherds are depicted as having pastoral concern for their sheep (Ps. 23; Jn. 10:1–18). They offer each member of their flock peace and security and protect them from harm. As a shepherd of lambs, you have a responsibility to protect those you serve.

Good practice must be an integral part of youth work and ministry. We should continually look for ways to improve the design and delivery of our programmes. The following guidance will help with this.

Risk assessment

There is no such thing as zero risk. Life is full of risk. For example, every car journey involves an element of risk. So does a walk into town. There are risks associated with staying indoors. However, that does not mean all risk is unavoidable. Most risk can be managed and measures taken to avoid or reduce the likelihood of harm. There is risk associated with youth work and ministry. You have a responsibility to create a safe environment for the young people you serve. They are far too precious to be exposed to harm, especially when it is unnecessary or avoidable.

Through good planning, vigilance and common sense you can reduce the risk of harm from preventable incidents. To do this you need to examine the hazards and likely risk. This is called 'Risk Assessment'. Hazards are anything that may cause harm. Examples might include loose cables, badly stacked chairs that could fall on people, poorly maintained vehicles, unhygienic catering facilities, excessive hours on duty, and violent intruders. Risk is the chance – high or low – that someone will be harmed by these hazards.

There are 5 stages to undertaking a risk assessment:

1. *Identify the hazards*
Look for potential hazards through all aspects of your youth work and ministry, including buildings and facilities, routine activities, transportation, residential experiences and staffing policies. Focus on the obvious, not the trivial. It is better to identify real and present dangers (such as fire due to inflammable materials being placed next to a cooker) than hypothetical and speculative perils (such as fire due to a plane crash). Risk assessment relies upon common sense.

2. *Identify those most at risk*
Determine who might be harmed by these potential hazards. They may include young people, youth workers, other centre users, or members of the general public. Decide how these people might be harmed by the identified hazards.

3. *Evaluate the risks*
Decide if current preventative measures are sufficient or if further action is required. Remember, you are unlikely to remove all risk. Is the risk high, medium or low? Determine if the ratio of volunteers and/or staff to young people is sufficient for a planned activity, and if they are adequately equipped, trained, qualified and/or experienced. This is particularly important when con-

sidering outdoor or residential activities, where special conditions apply. Draw up an action list of hazards that need corrective action.

4. Record your findings
It is important to make and keep notes. This demonstrates the importance you attach to risk assessment and enables you to demonstrate your actions.

5. Review your assessment
Because hazards and risks change over time, it is important to periodically review your risk assessment.

When you identify potential hazards, don't assume that others will deal with them. You have a responsibility to act. Can you safely neutralise the hazard? Do you need to move people to safety, or keep them away from the hazard? Who do you need to inform? Amaze, the Association of Christian Youth and Children's Workers, is a good source of information and advice. Their Best Practice Manual sets out the background to best practice in youth and children's work. Starting with the underpinning legal framework, it covers insurance, use of minibuses, child protection, health and safety, special needs, trips out and so on. Their contact details can be found in the Resource Directory at the back of this book.

To think about...
What are the risks currently associated with your practice? Think about building maintenance, fire safety, security, food standards and transportation. How do you manage these risks?

Child protection

There are numerous misconceptions that hinder our ability to protect young people from abuse. These include:

- Abuse doesn't happen in churches and certainly not in this one
- Christians don't do that sort of thing
- When you become a Christian your past is forgotten as well as forgiven
- Abuse only occurs in poor families.

Tragically, many abusers find the church an easy place in which to prey on young people and children. Too often, it is left to the media to remind us of the scale of the problem. On 31 March 2002, there were 25,700 people under 18 years old on the child protection register. This equates to 0.23 per cent of the British population.[2] Significantly many more cases go unreported.

Child protection is not a bureaucratic hindrance; it is a necessary and responsible response to the risks faced by today's young people. Abuse against young people is a serious matter and scars them for life. All those engaged in youth work and ministry have a duty to be vigilant. You need to know what to look out for and how to respond.

Types of abuse

We will look at four types of abuse. You may find some of the content disturbing, but it is important to understand what some of the young people we serve may have experienced. We will look at the signs of possible abuse. You need to know what to look out for whilst remembering that they are only indicators. Most can have a perfectly innocent explanation. Knowing what they are will help you build up a picture. It is important that these signs are not taken as an indication that abuse has taken place, but that we must be alert to the possibility.

1. *Physical abuse*

Physical abuse accounts for 19 per cent of all children on Britain's child protection register. It is defined as being actual, or likely, physical injury to a young person. It includes deliberate failure to prevent physical injury or suffering to a young person. It can include hitting, shaking, squeezing, burning, biting, administering poisonous substances, suffocating/drowning, or use of excessive force.

Signs to watch out for include: injuries not consistent with the explanation given; injuries to parts of the body not normally exposed to falls, rough games etc (e.g. back of the neck); injuries that have not received the medical attention you believe is required; reluctance to change for, or participate in, games or swimming; any signs of neglect (e.g. under-nourishment, abrasions etc).

2. *Sexual abuse*

Sexual abuse accounts for 10 per cent of those on the child protection register. It is defined as being actual, or likely, involvement of dependent, developmentally immature young people in sexual activity they do not fully comprehend or to which they are unable to give informed consent and which violate the social taboos of family roles.

Signs to watch out for include: excessive pre-occupation with sexual matters and detailed knowledge of adult sexual behaviour, or regular age-inappropriate sexual play; sexually provocative or seductive behaviour with adults; severe sleep disturbances with fears, phobias, vivid dreams or nightmares, sometimes with overt or veiled sexual connotations. It is normal for young people to explore and express their sexuality in ways that sometimes provoke or shock. In most cases this does not mean that sexual abuse has taken place.

3. *Neglect*

Neglect accounts for 39 per cent of those on the register. Given the right conditions, healthy organisms grow. If a plant is denied water or nutrients, it will soon look sickly. In the same way, a young person who is denied adequate food, shelter or hygiene will show the signs. Neglect is defined as persistent or severe neglect of a young person, or the failure to protect a young person from exposure to any kind of danger, including cold or starvation; or extreme failure to carry out important aspects of care, resulting in the significant impairment of the young person's health or development.

Signs to watch out for are the same as those for physical abuse.

4. *Emotional abuse*

Emotional abuse accounts for 17 per cent of children on the register. It is defined as being actual, or likely, severe adverse effect on the emotional development of a young person caused by persistent, or severe, emotional ill treatment or rejection. All abuse involves some emotional ill treatment.[3]

Signs to watch out for include: sudden changes or regression in mood or behaviour, particularly where a young person withdraws or becomes clinging; sudden nervousness or watchfulness; sudden under-achievement or lack of concentration; inappropriate relationships with peers and/or adults; extreme attention-seeking behaviour; persistent tiredness; persistent running away, stealing or lying.

To think about...
How does reviewing these types of abuse make you feel? Have you had experience in responding to child protection issues in your youth work and ministry?

Responding to abuse

Confronting possible abuse is difficult at the best of times. But it is imperative we respond in a calm and professional manner – not making a bad situation worse by clumsiness. This means being familiar with your church's child protection policy, which sets out the procedures you are expected to follow and the process by which the police and/or social services will be informed. All churches should have a child protection policy. This should include obtaining Enhanced Disclosure checks from the Criminal Records Bureau for all volunteers and staff, as well as church leaders. It is highly irresponsible to operate without this. The Churches' Child Protection Advisory Service offers training, guidance, resources and access to CRB Disclosure checks for churches. Details of how to contact them are in the Resource Directory at the back of this book.

The following guidance will help you implement your agreed policy. It does not replace it.

Disclosures

Your response will, in part, depend on the type of concern you have. When a young person tells you (discloses) they have been, or are being, subjected to possible abuse – or describes what you believe to be a potentially abusive situation – they are said to have made a disclosure. You have a moral and professional responsibility to act upon all disclosures (whether you believe them or not). Investigating the validity of a disclosure is the task of highly trained and experienced specialists. Your responsibility is simply to pass on information that will enable child protection experts to do their job well. When a young person makes a disclosure you have no choice, you must act. Your child protection policy will outline the procedures agreed by your church for informing social services and/or the police. Once a referral has been made, social services or the police will assume investigating responsibility. You will be required to cooperate with their enquiries.

There are a number of basic dos and don'ts. These include:

1. Do show the young person you take seriously what they are telling you. Respond, "I accept what you are saying." Make sure you give no sign of disbelieving them. Remember, it will have taken great courage to disclose such sensitive information. Do try to remain calm and be unshockable. Do give the young person your full attention, blocking out all distractions.

2. Don't push the young person for information or ask lots of questions. There must never be any suggestion that you put words into his or her mouth. Just let the young person say what they want.

   Don't promise complete confidentiality. You will need to pass on the disclosure to either social services or the police (more in Chapter 4).

3. Do make a full written record of the conversation, using abbreviations/initials, immediately afterwards and include as many facts and quotes as you can

recall – times, dates, places, names, etc. Always keep the original notes – even if you subsequently produce a neater version – and store them in a safe place.

4. Don't discuss the matter with anyone other than the police/social services and the child protection coordinator/advocate in your church/youth project. Don't inform the young person's parent(s)/carer(s) unless you are absolutely sure there is no possibility that they, or any relative/friend, could be involved and in cases of possible sexual abuse the parent(s)/carer(s) should never be informed. Anything that tips off the perpetrator damages the prospects of securing a criminal conviction. Don't make assumptions. Remember, you are most unlikely to be in possession of all the facts.

Suspicion

As painful as it is, dealing with a disclosure is relatively straightforward. The decision is made for you. However, deciding how to respond to a suspicion is far more complex. This involves judgement and wisdom. The following steps and questions will help you decide whether or not to act on a suspicion:

Consult the child protection coordinator/advocate in your church or call the Churches' Child Protection Advisory Service helpline (0845 120 4551). Is your suspicion shared by others? Keep a record of your suspicions and use it to detect patterns. Is it a recurring suspicion? Use sensitive questions to get at the cause of possible signs. Is it a suspicion that won't go away? If the answer is 'yes' then you should act on the suspicion as if it were a disclosure.

Avoiding confusion

Liberal use of common sense can avoid confusion. Think through your actions and how they will look through the eyes of an observer or 'unchurched' parent/carer. The following guidelines will protect you as much as the young people you serve.

1. If a colleague/team member appears to be behaving in inappropriate ways you owe it to them, as well as to the young people, to point out your concern. If your intervention is not accepted to your satisfaction you should advise your youth work coordinator or church leader.

2. Some people are more physically expressive than others. Furthermore, as a consequence of puberty, some young people can be flirtatious. Be extremely cautious about having any physical contact with the young people you serve. What you thought was an innocent side-on hug in the context of a group, might be interpreted by others as a sexual advance. If in any doubt, don't.

3. You should organize your work so that you are never alone with a young member of either sex. You should try to avoid giving young people lifts in your car. This has insurance implications and creates a risk. When this is unavoidable, you should ensure the last person dropped off is of the same sex as you. This may require a circuitous route.

4. You should be careful not to develop overly familiar relationships with the young people you serve, especially if and when communicating by email and mobile phone text. What you consider to be an innocent series

of communications could be interpreted as an attempt to groom a young person for sexual exploitation (soon to be a criminal offence[4]).

Discipline

Maintaining effective discipline is important. First, it promotes safety, reducing the risk of accidents and injuries to young people and youth workers as a result of careless or deliberate action. Young people and youth workers have a right to exist in a safe environment. Second, it promotes respect for self and others. It values the inherent worth of individuals as those made in the image of God (Gen. 1:27; Eph. 2:10). Young people and youth workers have a right to exist in an intimidation-free environment. Third, it promotes growth, enabling young people to gain more from the educational process that is youth work and ministry. Young people and youth workers have a right to exist in a positive learning environment.

Effective discipline requires you to display:

1. *Consistency*
   Young people have a heightened sense of justice. Ask yourself, 'Am I responding differently to this person?'

2. *Proportionality*
   Before Moses was given the Law, there was lawlessness. In the chaos of compensation hell it was a situation of give them an inch and they'll take a mile, or demand an optician in payment for the loss of an eye, and a dentist for a tooth. God introduced the Law to restrain the effects of anti-social behaviour. It became limited to

'take … eye for eye, tooth for tooth' (Ex. 21:24; Lev. 24:20; Deut. 19:21). Ask yourself, am I responding too harshly? Never respond out of frustration or anger. Ask yourself, am I responding too quickly or aggressively?

3. Self-control

Never use any form of physical restraint or aggression. It is nearly always indefensible. The only exception is when it is absolutely necessary in order to protect yourself or others from significant physical harm. You will then be required to justify your judgment – probably in a court of law. If you or others feel threatened, dial 999 and ask for the police. Ask yourself, am I responding too physically?

4. Love

Effective discipline is a demonstration of true love (Heb. 12:10–11). It always seeks opportunities to restore people to a right relationship with self, others and God (Mt. 18:15–17). Ask yourself, am I responding from a motive that wants the best for the young person?

Steve is 15 years old and often described as being a 'lively' young man. His behaviour has got steadily worse over the last six months. At first he simply opted out of certain group activities, saying they were boring and childish. But now he is becoming verbally aggressive towards young people and youth workers alike. Some quieter members of the group have expressed their frustration to you. One or two have stopped coming altogether as a consequence. Despite being very negative about the group, Steve continues to attend – though less frequently than before. Steve's parents both attend church; his dad is the treasurer. Last week, a window was broken and the suspicion points to Steve.

To think about:
If Steve were in your youth group, how would you respond – and why?

The next chapter, 'Working with individuals', will look at how to connect with young people, the art of listening, and issues of confidentiality, referral and prayer ministry. This will enable you to forge strong relationships with individual young people.

Summary

- Just because most youth work and ministry is volunteer-led does not mean it can be unprofessional.
- You have a responsibility to create a safe environment for the young people you serve, working in accordance with statutory legislation and responsible self-regulation.
- Through good planning, vigilance and common sense you can reduce the risk of harm from preventable incidents. This requires use of 'risk assessment'.
- There are four types of abuse: physical abuse, sexual abuse, neglect and emotional abuse. Each has signs to look out for.
- You need to act on all disclosures, reporting them to either social services or the police.
- Effective discipline helps promote safety, respect, growth and education. To be effective, discipline must be consistent, proportional, self-controlled, non-physical and loving.

Notes

1. *The Times Magazine*, 28 June 2003, p.9
2. Home Office figures.
3. Statistics from the Department of Health, which says the remaining 15 per cent belong in a new category of 'mixed/not recommended'.
4. At the time of publication, the Sexual Offences Bill was nearing the end of its passage through the British Parliament.

PART TWO

WORKING

4

Working with individuals

In the film *Mr Holland's Opus*,[1] the lifelong ambition of Glen Holland (Richard Dreyfuss) is to write a major opus. As a financially struggling composer, he is forced to teach music in an inner-city school to young people with no apparent interest or aptitude. It is deeply frustrating for Mr Holland to have his passion permanently ridiculed, but he persists. He eventually stops seeing the children in his class as pupils, and comes to know them as people with real-life stories, struggles and potentials. He starts to invest his time and energy in the young people, spending hours teaching them to see beyond the notes in the score and feel the music. It is no easy task, but in true Hollywood tradition the inner-city young people develop remarkable musicality. And what is more important, they gain self-esteem.

Mr Holland makes a real difference in their lives, but on the day he retires he still hasn't written his major opus. He has invested all of his time and energy into successive generations of young people, leaving nothing for his own ambitions. His lifetime aspiration unfulfilled, he feels like a musical failure. On the last day at school, pupils past and present gather to show their appreciation by performing his unfinished opus. Mr Holland's true opus is not on the

sheets of music he has written but in the young people
he has served.

Mr Holland's Opus gives an insight into the world
of youth work and ministry. Success as a volunteer
youth worker rests not so much on your knowledge of
the Christian faith as on your ability to establish and
maintain effective relationships with young people. This
requires you to overcome your prejudices and fears, and
invest your time and energy into individuals and groups
of young people.

Building positive relationships with young people is
fundamental to youth work and ministry. Some mistakenly
believe that youth work and ministry is little more than
organising activities for young people. They are wrong.
The values of voluntary participation, informal education,
empowerment, equality of opportunity and incarnation
(see Chapter 1) challenge this. Others talk of 'relational'
youth work as if there is an alternative. There is no such
thing as non-relational youth work and ministry.

The message of the Bible is that God the Father, God
the Son and God the Holy Spirit exist together in perfect
relationship. The Trinity invites us – despite all our imper-
fections – to experience a new quality of relationship with
God and each other that we could not otherwise attain.
Youth work and ministry provides young people with an
opportunity to experience positive relationships with their
peers and ultimately with God. Your role as a volunteer
is to model this possibility.

Connecting

Connecting is the doorway to lasting relationships. It is
the initial encounter, the first few conversations between
youth worker and young person. Some find the prospect

of striking up a conversation with a young person so daunting they shy away from youth work and ministry. Let's look at why this happens and how you can establish effective connections with young people.

Connecting can be daunting

Connecting with young people can sometimes appear daunting.

Firstly, we may fear that young people will ridicule, reject or worse still ignore our approach. During these moments, personal insecurities developed during our own childhood or adolescence rise to the surface. We react. To protect ourselves from painful memories we avoid situations that remind us of our vulnerability.

Secondly, we may avoid young people because we are not used to connecting with them. We become fearful of the unknown. Alternatively, we may be influenced by negative stereotypes of young people as all aggressive, rude and uncommunicative.

Thirdly, we may feel ill-equipped, believing that we lack the inter-personal skills necessary to initiate contact with young people. A few people do indeed lack these skills. But for the vast majority, deficiencies can be overcome with increased confidence, experience and training.

It is amazing just how many negative thoughts stop us from doing even the simplest of tasks. Think back to the first time you entered a youth club as an adult. How did you feel? The hardest part is always overcoming our own fears and ignorance. Once the initial contact is made, the rest becomes easier.

To think about...
What was your first experience as a youth
worker of connecting with young people?
Was it easy or hard? How receptive were
the young people? If you have been involved
in youth work and ministry for some time,
what if anything do you do differently now
when connecting with young people?

How to make connections

Connecting with young people can be daunting, but the
following tips will help you to be more effective.

1. Decide to connect

Connecting with young people starts with a conscious
decision to get involved. Be ready to make the most of
opportunities that arise. There is rarely a perfect time
to connect with young people. Ask the Holy Spirit to
guide you. Don't wait for young people to take the
initiative. They may want to connect with you but not
know how. You may be surprised how open young
people are towards you.

2. Take the initiative

Observe where young people are and go to them. If
you work in a building, where do the young people
congregate (main hall, corridor, entrance, car park)? If
your work is outside (outreach or detached), where do
the different groups of young people hang out (high
street, park, waste land, estate)? Be prepared to take
the initiative.

3. *Be consistent*
Positive relationships are built on quantity time, not just quality time. This means you being consistent in your attendance and participation. When you connect with a young person, make it a habit to renew the rapport when you meet again. If you meet in a different setting (e.g. shopping mall or church), make sure you acknowledge the connection there as well.

4. *Be a good guest*
The first few times I visit your house I am conscious of being a guest in your space. I note your customs (e.g. taking shoes off in the house), the spoken and unspoken rules (e.g. no smoking) and who appears to be the dominant figure (e.g. the dog). If I turn up at your door unannounced and uninvited I am even more aware that I am a prospective guest.

To connect with a young person is to enter their domain. Remember, you are a guest. This has little to do with who owns the building you are in. And a lot to do with relationships – and they control who enters and who doesn't. To be allowed in, you need to earn the right to be on their territory: you can't force your way in, and you mustn't outstay your welcome. You should discover the customs and rules of their space and the main characters.

5. *Be chatty*
Aim to create dialogue with young people, not deliver a monologue at them. A relationship can't flourish when one partner consistently monopolises the conversation. Look for common ground. Jesus was accomplished at this. He used everyday cultural interests such as fishing, banquets, feasting and farming to relate to people. Don't be afraid to show your ignorance of their interests.

It is better to ask dumb questions than to be labelled a fraud. Sometimes young people say or do things purely to test your commitment to them, so it is important to be accepting. Remember, God is the judge – not you. Jesus demonstrated that God is often more generous and non-judgmental than we are.

6. Be yourself

Nothing is so obvious or off-putting as mutton dressed up as lamb. Don't be anything other than yourself. Your primary task is not to be the sharpest dressed or best skateboarder, but to form positive relationships with young people. Many young people feel pressured to compete with their peers, and they don't need the further pressure of having to compete with their youth worker as well. There is nothing quite so powerful as an adult who takes a healthy interest in the lives of young people. Ultimately, youth workers are not remembered for their dress sense or ability to skate, but for the time and energy they invest into the lives of young people. Let the presence of God be an attractive witness. Jesus said: "Let your light shine before men, that they may see your good deeds and praise your Father in heaven." (Mt. 5:16) Let your integrity draw young people towards God.

Going Deeper

Your purpose in connecting with young people is to offer them opportunities to go deeper, understanding more about themselves, others and God. It is only as they go deeper that they begin to address issues of concern to them. Without this, your practice would be irrelevant.

The Relationship Triangle (below) shows the progression from initial connection, to positive relationship, pastoral support and ultimately, for some, lasting change.

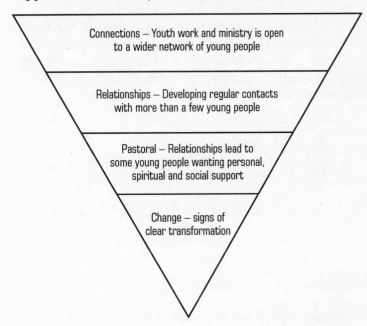

Connections – Youth work and ministry is open to a wider network of young people

Relationships – Developing regular contacts with more than a few young people

Pastoral – Relationships lead to some young people wanting personal, spiritual and social support

Change – signs of clear transformation

Each level of the Relationship Triangle represents a different stage of relational progression. In Level 1, you connect with a diverse range of individuals and groups of young people. This comprises the first few conversations. Some connections with young people go no further than this. In Level 2, you begin to establish regular contact with individuals and groups of young people, and positive relationships start to form. Common interests, shared activities and quality time all provide a context for positive relationships to flourish. In Level 3, some young people begin to make use of the pastoral support you offer. You become a resource and means of support, whilst ensuring you do not create an unhealthy dependence upon you. By

Level 4, some young people display clear signs of change. This transformation is brought about by the voluntary response young people make to what they have seen in you.

As the Relationship Triangle gets narrower, the focus shifts from quantity of connection to quality of change. Inevitably you will connect with a large number of young people, but invest quality time with a smaller number of individuals who choose to go deeper with you.

To think about...
Think about the young people you serve. Which level in the Relationship Triangle best describes your position with them? What would it take for you and the young people to move to the next level?

Listening

Listening is one of the key skills in youth work and ministry. A recent NSPCC poster campaign featured a child that was obviously in trouble. The caption read, 'What he needs is a good listening to.' Unfortunately, being listened to has become one of life's luxuries.

Among Christians, evangelicals are often portrayed as being quick to speak and slow to listen. In the Old Testament, Job's life was full of struggles and pain. His three friends were quick to recognise this, but instead of rushing in with words of comfort and counsel they sat in silence with him (Job 2:11–13). For seven days they listened to Job. Listening can be a profound ministry. James says, 'Everyone should be quick to listen, slow to speak and slow to become angry, …' (Jas. 1:19)

Listening skills

Listening is not easy. We live in a world full of distractions and noise. Hearing and listening are not the same things – it is quite possible to hear someone speak without actually listening to them. Here are some tips to help you improve your listening skills:

1. Make a conscious decision to be an active listener. This requires concentration and time.
2. Don't use the time while the other person is speaking to plan your reply.
3. Listen with all your senses: with your eyes as well as your ears. What is the person communicating with their body language, facial expression and/or appearance? What are they not saying?
4. Maintain good eye contact with the person you are listening to – though do not intimidate by staring.
5. Don't fear silence. Don't fill gaps with nervous or self-centred chatter. The young person you are listening to may need this time to gather their thoughts.
6. Because some young people find prolonged silence intimidating, be prepared to ask open questions that enable them to enter or maintain the conversation. That is, questions that can't be answered with a simple 'yes' or 'no' e.g. 'What did you mean by ...'
7. Without interrupting, ask occasional questions that show you are interested and convey support.
8. Periodically, repeat back to the person you are listening to what you have heard them say. 'What I have heard you say so far is... .' This shows that you are concentrating; ensures you have heard correctly; and allows the person being listened to, to amend their words if necessary.
9. Be slow to give answers. The aim is not for you to prove

your worth by dispensing quick-fix responses but rather for the young person to understand their own questions and then go exploring answers. Use questions to help the young person reflect and explore their options.

To think about...
How comfortable do you feel with listening?
How can you improve your listening skills?

Confidentiality

As a youth worker, you may find that young people treat you like a priest. They tell you sensitive information on the assumption that you are bound by a strict code of confidentiality that prevents you from telling anyone else. Youth work and ministry certainly must provide young people with a safe context in which to say things they might not want to say to peers, parents or others. Children of church-attending parents/guardians do not always find the church or youth group a safe place. As well as being their youth worker, you may also be a potential informer. Can the young people speak freely without fear of it reaching their parents? It is always important to remember, your primary contract is with the young people – not their parents.

It is also important to foster a relationship of trust with the young people you serve, but this may create difficult ethical dilemmas. For example, what if a young person tells you they intend to harm themselves or someone else? Are you legally obliged to inform others? And if so, who?

To think about...
Have you been put in a difficult position because of something a young person said to you? How did you deal with this?

Current British law only requires citizens to report acts of suspected terrorism and imposes a statutory duty only on social services departments and their staff – not others – to act on cases of possible abuse. Whilst there is no legal requirement to pass on confidential information – even when a child or young person is at risk of significant harm – there can sometimes be a strong moral obligation to act.

You should never promise absolute confidentiality. To protect the welfare of young people, or others, it may occasionally be necessary to pass on information to appropriate third parties. You do not create trust by breaking promises, no matter how justified you may feel. To avoid misunderstanding, the boundaries of confidentiality should be made clear before there is a possibility of sensitive information being disclosed. It is good practice to include a confidentiality statement on the youth group's printed programme and display it prominently where the group meets. A confidentiality statement could simply say: As youth workers, we will never gossip to others what you say to us in private. We shan't keep a confidence if in our opinion this places you or someone else at risk of significant harm. For your sake, we might then have a responsibility to inform a third party.

It is important for you to distinguish between the role of a youth worker and that of a counsellor. Youth work and ministry is not a counselling service, and you are not a counsellor. This is a highly specialised skill and the

title conveys a level of training that as a volunteer youth
worker you are unlikely to have had.

Referral

It may sometimes be necessary to pass on one of the young
people you serve to another person or agency for more
specialist support. This process is called referral. Referral
is appropriate in a number of situations. Firstly, if the
young person specifically requests that they be referred
to someone else. Secondly, if you – or your organisation – do not have the skills, knowledge or experience
required to adequately support the young person. Finally,
referral is appropriate if you believe there is a legal or
moral requirement to involve another agency; normally
because the young person – or someone else – is at risk
of serious harm.

Referral demonstrates the respect you have for the
young person concerned. It is not an admission of failure or
inadequacy. Referral requires your continued support and
often your involvement as well. It is not a way to off-load
a young person onto someone else. Referral requires the
mutual agreement of young person and youth worker. It
is not your chance to impose your will on others.

Referral requires you to be aware of some of the external
agencies available to young people in your community.
You should not attempt to refer only to Christian agencies,
as some churches are in the habit of doing. This rarely
provides young people with the quality of service they
require and demonstrates a lack of self-understanding
and respect for others.

Local referral agencies

There are hundreds of possible local and national agencies to whom you can refer young people for specialised support. Examples include Connexions, counselling agencies, doctors, drug action teams, police, pregnancy advice centres, schools, social services, and numerous telephone help lines such as Childline (0800 1111) or The Samaritans (08457 90 90 90). Useful numbers are included in the Resource Directory at the back of this book. Consider providing all young people with a list of useful contact numbers.

Prayer ministry

Youth work and ministry enables young people to experience change. Sometimes this is brought about by their response to the creative and educative programme you offer. Other times, it is due to God's divine intervention in their lives – and the responses they choose to make to him.

Prayer is an important element of youth work and ministry. You will obviously want to pray for the young people you serve, remembering them in your private devotions. There will also be times when it is appropriate for you to pray directly with the young people. This gives them an opportunity to experience the power of prayer and to observe a model of spirituality that they may choose to adopt for themselves.

Some Christian youth workers are too reticent to offer prayer, and so restrict young people's spiritual development. Others are too forceful, imposing prayer upon young people in a form of religious abuse. The following guidelines will enable you to maintain an effective prayer ministry:

1. Be enthusiastic to pray for – or better still, with – young people whilst being respectful of their wishes if they

decline your offer. Ask yourself: Do they want to receive prayer?

2. Be specific about prayer needs. Ask the young person: What are they wanting you to pray?

3. Be alert, keeping your eyes open at all times when praying for the young person. Ask God: What is happening?

4. Be wise. Where possible, only pray with someone of the same gender. Keep physical contact to a minimum and use no physical contact when praying with the opposite gender or if you are not directly observable by others. Ask yourself: If someone were to walk in now, how might this look?

5. Be empowering, inviting the person you are praying with to participate in some form of response or prayer. Before praying, always explain what you are about to do and afterwards, what happened. Invite the person being prayed for to respond in your prayer.

6. Be expectant, believing that God wants to work in both you and the young person you are praying with. Sometimes this will happen quietly, other times dramatically. Ask God: Will you meet this young person's need(s)?

In Chapter Five, 'Working with groups', we will look at some of the skills involved in leading or facilitating small groups and cells. This will enable you to be a more effective group worker. But before then, let's recap on what we have covered in this chapter:

Summary

● Youth work and ministry is formed on the quality of relationships between youth workers and young people.

- Connecting comprises the initial contact and first few conversations.
- Going deeper enables young people to explore issues of concern to them in more meaningful ways. It opens up the possibility of lasting change.
- Listening skills are essential and have to be practised as listening is qualitatively different to hearing.
- Confidentiality is important and should be maintained where possible but it can never be guaranteed.
- Referral to specialist agencies is sometimes appropriate when young people require more than we are able to offer them.
- Effective prayer ministry offers young people the opportunity to experience the power of prayer and must always be undertaken with wisdom and sensitivity.

NOTES

1. *Mr Holland's Opus* © 1995, Hollywood Pictures.

5

Working with groups

Two seemingly unconnected strands of my life recently came together in a bizarre way.

Strand One. Shortly after I moved from London to the Black Country[1] in the heart of England, my car was bitten by a prowling lion. (Oh, how the children screamed as they stared into its gaping mouth and counted its sharp white teeth.) Then I was woken up in the night by an earthquake measuring 4.8 on the Richter scale (please, no more 'did the earth move for you?' jokes). OK, so the lion was at the West Midlands Safari Park and the earthquake was much too feeble to cause wide scale structural damage. To my London friends, who think I have moved out of the cultural and political metropolis into the land that time forgot, it sounded dramatic.

Strand Two. I am a lifelong supporter of West Ham Football Club in East London. I've been singing "I'm forever blowing bubbles" since they won the FA Cup in 1975. At a distance people assume I support the Birmingham club Aston Villa, which due to a lack of imagination copied West Ham's claret and blue shirt design.

Part of the reason for moving to the Black Country was to rejoin Chawn Hill Christian Centre. I am now an 'extra timer' in the church where I started out as a 'full timer'.

Here is the bizarre connection. I'm not the only West Ham supporter in my church. First there was Mike and his son, Sam. Then Steve came along, followed shortly by Adam. With me, there are five of us. This may not seem much to the hundreds of Manchester United fans who live anywhere but Manchester, but five West Ham supporters outside of East London accounts for almost all of us. With our claret and blue shirts – and depressed faces – we are a recognisable group. The last time West Ham played at West Bromwich Albion (the local team), we five defiantly wore our shirts on a train packed with thousands of rival fans. We were a group.

In this chapter we shall consider the significance of groups for young people, how to identify the roles that different group members perform and how to manage the ensuing group dynamics. We shall also look at your approach to leading or facilitating your small or cell group, which first we need to define.

Introducing groups

All youth work and ministry involves group work. This is the process of engaging with identified groups of young people. Some group work is informal and/or temporary. It is based on conversations with a group of young people who regularly 'hang out' on a street corner, or the *ad hoc* participation of a group in a time-limited task.

Other group work is more formal and/or permanent. It involves the structured organisation of people or members into recognised groups. Such groups come in a range of shapes and sizes, but all aim to provide an intimate environment in which each young person knows, and is known by, a handful of peers and a designated leader or facilitator.

Small or cell groups provide a supportive and creative environment that enables young people to discover and realise their God-given potential. Small or cell group ministries are those that grow through multiplication. The enlisting of new members leads to the creation of new small or cell groups, not the enlargement of the original group. Consequently, small or cell groups work in organisations of any size. They enable modestly sized youth ministries to grow numerically, and big youth ministries to grow relationally. Six people can form one small or cell group; sixty can form up to ten groups.

For a more detailed look at types of groups, and cells in particular, please see *Growing Community: Making Groups Work with Young People.*[2]

Cell church principles

Cell groups are a particular type of small group used by cell churches. Cells are not viewed as a supplement to the big group or church gathering but as the basic building block. Just as the life of the human body is in the cells, so the life of a cell church is found in the cell groups. The big group is formed by all the cells coming together, and is supplementary to the essential cell groups. Cell group meetings are often structured around the four Ws: welcome, worship, word and witness.

1. Welcome
An initial welcoming 'icebreaker' helps members get to know each other and relax into the setting.

2. Worship
A participatory act of creative worship enables members to focus on getting to know God better.

3. *Word*
   An application-centred ministry time rather than a Bible study, usually tackling a single issue or question.

4. *Witness*
   An opportunity for cell members to pray for their non-Christian friends, and plan ways of sharing their faith with others.

To think about…
What has been your experience, to date, of small or cell groups? How – if at all – have you found them?

Group members

During the 1970s, Hollywood was fascinated with disaster movies. Planes crashed, buildings burnt, ocean liners sank, dams burst, cable cars jammed and earthquakes shook but it was the eclectic cast of characters that made these films so entertaining. They all had very different temperaments and personalities. Emotional sparks flew with every new explosion.

Believing they were all going to die, *Joker* would sit in the corner clutching a bottle of whisky and cracking terrible jokes. *Negative* was essentially a coward who rejected all escape plans and violently clashed with their source, *Captain Sensible*. After an hour, *Martyr* would sign his own death certificate by revealing a shameful secret that inevitably meant he had to be killed while performing some remarkably daring but suicidal feat. Taking charge of the group would be *Reluctant Hero*, who, incidentally, was always male. He would be the one who calmed the group and brought about their dramatic rescue, ably assisted by his female lead, *Miss Unflappable* (with the flapping eyes and torn, flowing dress). After ninety minutes, all but *Martyr* would emerge alive to star in another disaster.

Most small or cell groups have an equally strong cast of diverse characters. Understanding group dynamics will help you be a better group leader or facilitator.

Spud's 8

Imagine that Spud leads a small or cell group of eight young people. Each is a strong character. Let's take a close look at the characters that together form Spud's group. You will recognise some of your own young people in these characters, but remember that not all the roles are found in all groups. Also, some young people have the ability to play more than one role so you may need to combine two or more characters to form one actual personality.

1. Dominator

She always manages to be the centre of attention. If someone has a question, she has an answer. When someone makes a statement, she cuts in with her own, often unrelated, utterance. She has 'been there and done that' before anyone else has even thought about it. Her voice is loud, and her body language louder still. If only Dominator would listen to what others have to say. Yet Dominator helps the group to coalesce. Her presence gives value to the other members, who like to be associated with such a confident person.

2. Spectator

He sits at the edge of the room, near the exit. He is content to watch what the rest of the group is doing. Only a mind-reader could tell whether his silence results from profound boredom, intense interest or an

inability to make himself heard. He never contributes
to a discussion, and direct questions receive a minimal
response. If only Spectator would say something. Yet
Spectator may be deciding whether this is a safe group
to join. Alternatively, he may be content to let others
speak first.

3. *Gladiator*

She loves a fight, and she doesn't care with whom or
about what. But she is inarticulate. In a heated debate,
she quickly gets frustrated by her inability to express
herself adequately. She often feels threatened by those
she perceives as superior to herself, and when cornered
she lashes out. She deals with this by running away,
either physically or emotionally, and seeking solitude.
If only Gladiator would take a deep breath and get a
grip on her emotions. Yet Gladiator is good at standing
up for people, and will often be fiercely loyal to those
who are vulnerable. She can be a comforting presence
in a hostile world.

4. *Placator*

He runs around after Gladiator. He hates conflict, and
will do everything possible to ensure nothing is ever
said. He prefers to sweep things under the carpet rather
than deal with them in the open. He can appear anxious
and overly concerned that the group will fall apart. If
only Placator would say what he really thought. Yet
Placator is very good at uniting the group; after all,
someone needs to keep the peace. He is highly sensitive
to other people's feelings and is a good listener.

5. *Motivator*

She is an idealist in need of a cause. Individuals take
second place as she pushes on towards her goal. Sitting

down to discuss endless questions is a waste of time – there is real work to be done. Motivator can appear pious and intimidate the rest of the group (not to mention the group leader). If only Motivator would stop being so perfect. Yet it is Motivator who often reminds the group of its mission.

6. *Terminator*
Faced with optimism, Terminator takes it upon himself to inject a touch of realism. Positive suggestions are met with ten reasons why they won't work. His pessimism and disinterest can dampen the enthusiasm of newcomers. He doesn't even have to speak; his body language says it all. If only Terminator would think positively. Yet Terminator may sometimes be right. Not every idea is appropriate, and even the good ones have flaws. By identifying problems, he ensures that others can solve them.

7. *Orator*
Just when a discussion gets interesting, Orator diverts attention with an unrelated statement or question. Not only that, she doesn't know when to stop talking. Running out of intelligent things to say doesn't seem to help. When she gets going, everyone else gives up. She has a theory about almost everything and even an opinion about opinionated people. If only Orator would stop talking. Yet whenever there is an awkward silence, Orator gets a discussion going. She is often able to introduce lateral or 'deeper' thoughts, to the benefit of the rest of the group.

8. *Actor*
All the world's a stage for Actor. One minute he can be playing a 'funny' part, the next it's a 'straight' role. Actor

rarely accepts a walk-on part. A passionate being, he is either up or down but never in between. When the atmosphere becomes too intense or challenging for him, he diverts attention with a quick gag. This prevents the conversation from getting serious. If only Actor would be himself. Yet Actor is great fun to be with and adept at helping others to feel relaxed, particularly those who don't want to take centre stage themselves.

Part of your role as group leader/facilitator is to help members gain a better understanding of themselves and others. Each of the eight characters in Spud's group makes both positive and negative contributions to group life. People's weaknesses are often their strengths, and vice versa. If you react against the negative, you may repress the positive.

To think about...
Which of the eight characters in Spud's cell group do you recognise as being part of your small or cell group? What impact do these characters have on your group?

Managing group dynamics

Leading a group of diverse characters can sometimes be difficult. The following tips will enable you to better manage the characters in your group, enabling you to get the most out of Orator, Gladiator and Motivator.

1. *Affirmation*
Some people react strongly because of low self-worth. Orator's incessant talking may indicate she needs praise for her 'worthy' contribution. Gladiator may defend

the weak because she wants to feel needed. As group leader/facilitator, you should always seek to affirm group members – even when they give what others consider to be a wrong answer.

2. *Questions*

Well-crafted questions have a profound effect on a small group. As group leader/facilitator, use questions to stimulate discussion, draw others in and stimulate enquiry. Questions should be clear and designed to confirm what people know rather than expose what they don't. Only ask questions the group has a realistic chance of answering.

Not all questions are helpful. Which of these two questions is better – and why? "Does anyone here watch television?" or "Placator, why do you watch television?" There are only two answers to the first question – Yes or No. It neither stimulates discussion nor is targeted at anyone in particular. The second question is more likely to get a response that will open up discussion.

3. *Seating*

Room layout affects group dynamics. A small room with easy chairs will create a different dynamic to a large hall with plastic chairs set in rows. As group leader/facilitator, you should aim to sit next to Gladiator so subtle use of body language can both reassure and restrain her. Equally, you should sit opposite Spectator so you can draw him in. Remember the importance of eye contact and make sure everyone is within winking distance of each other. If necessary, invite those on the fringe to move in.

4. *Body language*

The way you stand, what you do with your hands and

where you look all help to tell a story. For example;
glancing at the clock, doodling on a pad or yawning
all communicate lack of interest. An awareness of body
language will enable you to manage the signals you
send to others and interpret those they send back to
you. As group leader/facilitator, you can use body language to draw people into a discussion and, if necessary,
silence others. To manage Dominator, make direct eye
contact with her and then deliberately switch your focus
to Spectator. Repeat this until both get the message. If
necessary, hold your hand up to Dictator and signal to
Spectator – as if you were directing traffic.

5. *Direct intervention*

There will be times when Dominator and Orator do not
respond to subtle interventions and, for the sake of the
whole group, you will need to take more decisive action.
Try applying all the above measures in one sweeping
action, saying something like, "David, thank you for
your contribution. I appreciate all you have to say, and
can we now open up the discussion? Maria, what do
you think?"

As you do so, lean away from David and towards
Maria, using your hands to gently direct the discussion traffic. Notice how 'and' is far more constructive
than 'but'.

Group leadership

As a leader or facilitator, you have significant influence on
the small or cell group you serve. If you are friendly and
open, the group is more likely to be friendly and warm.
It is your responsibility to care for the young people in
your small or cell group. You are the youth work and

ministry as far as they are concerned. Equally, the role you adopt will also influence the group. There are different approaches to leadership. Some people adopt a more authoritarian approach, giving instructions for people to follow. Others adopt a more participatory approach, enabling people to determine their own actions.

As with Spud's eight characters, let's look at five leadership styles.

1. **Dictator:** *'You listen; I make the decisions'*
   He takes control of the group because he knows what is best. He doesn't waste time asking people what they think because he already knows the answer. It is he who determines what the group will do, when and where. He asks the questions and gives the answers, but in reality spends more time making statements. As leader, he retains total control of the group.

2. **Negotiator:** *'I listen; I make the decisions'*
   She accepts responsibility for the group and is prepared to make the difficult decisions. However, she is keen for group members to influence her. She asks questions because she is genuinely interested in what people have to say. She will sometimes let the group make a decision for themselves, but only on minor matters. As leader, she negotiates with those less powerful than herself.

3. **Participator:** *'We listen; we make the decisions'*
   He considers himself a member of the group. Decisions are made collectively, with everyone given equal opportunity to influence the final outcome. Responsibility is shared equally between all members, and it is at this level that he contributes. He does not control the agenda, and group members are free to ask questions of anyone

about anything. They may choose to recognise him as their leader but are always free to change their minds. As leader, he is an equal stakeholder.

4. Facilitator: *'We listen; you make the decisions'*
She aims to serve the group, of which she is not an equal member. The group members are responsible for directing their own affairs, and her charge is to help them be self-sufficient. As someone slightly detached from the group she brings suggestions and occasionally an alternative perspective, but she is careful not to impose her own values. As leader, she is a less-than-equal adviser.

5. Spectator: *'I listen; you make the decisions'*
His presence may provide some initial reassurance, but the group is not reliant upon him. They make all their own decisions, leaving him to observe – but not interfere. As leader, he has no need for power.

No one approach is inherently right or wrong. Each small or cell group requires its own approach. As leader or facilitator, you should adopt the style that suits the current needs of your small or cell group. For example, the early stages of a small-group cycle usually require a more directive approach, but as group members develop this may become too restrictive. They will then require a more hands-off approach. As leader or facilitator, you should aim for your group members to be self-determining at the earliest opportunity. This means providing increasing opportunities for shared responsibility and supporting them in their learning process.

> **To think about...**
> What role are you currently performing in the small or cell group you serve? On reflection, what role does the group need you to perform – and why?

The following chapter, 'Working more effectively', offers you a well-earned break from the skills and methods of youth work and ministry. Instead, we shall focus on you. Reflection, character, spirituality and belonging are all important characteristics of an 'extra-timer'. This will enable you to sustain your involvement and be effective with young people. But until then, here's a recap of what we have covered in this chapter.

Summary

- Almost all youth work and ministry involves some form of group work.
- Small or cell groups provide a structured approach to group work, ensuring that every young person knows and is known by a handful of peers and a designated leader or facilitator.
- Groups comprise a diverse range of characters, each capable of making both positive and negative contributions.
- Challenging group dynamics can be better managed with affirmation, questions, seating, body language and direct intervention.
- The role of the group leader or facilitator needs to change according to the needs of the group.

NOTES

1. Though the precise boundary is hotly disputed, as a generalisation
   the Black Country is the area covered by the Metropolitan Boroughs of
   Dudley, Sandwell, Walsall and Wolverhampton to the south and west of
   Birmingham.
2. Brierley, D. (2003), *Growing Community: Making Groups Work with
   Young People*, Carlisle: Authentic

6

Working more effectively

Z had problems. He had a fear of enclosed spaces and crowds, and he struggled with intense feelings of inadequacy. Z decided to see a therapist. Perhaps this would help him make sense of life. So Z laid back on the couch and spoke about his anxious childhood: how his mother had never had time for him, how his father flew the nest when he was just a youngster, and what it felt like to be the middle child in a large family with millions of brothers and sisters. Z had never felt that anyone paid him any attention as a child. Life as an adult wasn't any better. He had entered the work force as a manual labourer – despite his inability to lift more than ten times his own body weight. Now, in later life, Z was concerned about his own needs. The whole system made him feel so inadequate – as if he were an ant. But that was the problem; Z was an ant!

Like Z, in the film *Antz*,[1] it is easy to get caught up in the busy routine of life, never taking time to think about what it is you do and why. As an 'extra timer', you juggle relationships, work commitments and chores with your youth work and ministry. Sometimes your own needs appear to be get squeezed out. But you're just a volunteer, right?

You are not just a volunteer youth worker. As an 'extra-timer', you invest your spare time and energy into the lives of young people in your community. This is something to be proud of. Though not all young people will thank you each week for your time and energy, most will be profoundly influenced by what you offer them. You make a real difference to their lives.

You are not just a volunteer youth worker. You are also a human being. You are not merely a human resource to be expended for the sake of young people, or even the Christian faith. You are a beautiful human being who is made in the image of God. Just as Christ needed rest (Lk. 8:23; Jn. 4:6), friends (Mt. 11:19; Jn. 13:23; 15:15) and time alone (Mk. 1:35; 6:46–47) so too do you. Give yourself some respect. Make space for yourself and others. Sometimes you will need to say 'no'. If it helps, by doing this you will model to young people what it means to live a more balanced human life – as God intended.

In this chapter, we will take a break from looking at the skills of youth work and ministry to consider some of the inner qualities that are required. This is less about 'doing' and more about 'being'. We shall look at the importance of your reflection, character, spirituality and belonging.

Reflection

Frogs are sensible enough to not jump into boiling water. However, an urban legend says that if you put a frog into cold water and gradually heat the water, the frog will not appreciate the danger in time and be boiled to death. Failure to identify change in its environment and respond accordingly results in the frog's demise. In fact, frogs aren't really this daft. When it gets too hot they leap out. This is not an experiment to try at home, Blue Peter viewers – at least not without the informed consent of the frog or its parent/guardian. I use this legend to illustrate the importance of reflection.

Reflection is the ability to mentally step outside of a situation and see things differently. It digs beneath the surface to explore hidden events, motives and needs. Reflective practice is concerned not so much with what happens as how and why it happens. Consequently, it aids our understanding and ability to solve problems.

1. *Reflection brings about learning from everyday experiences*

Life is full of events, many of them unrelated. It is easy to miss what is going on around us. How many times do you have to drive down the same road before you notice the overgrown garden belonging to the elderly couple? Or how frequently the convenience store has boarded-up windows? Observing one aspect of life can result in new understanding in another.

While writing this I became distracted by an encounter between two cats. Despite their confrontational body language and wails, both clearly didn't want to fight. They'd fought over the neutrality of my garden so many times I imagined they privately thought it was all rather futile. And yet neither wanted to be the first to back down. Eventually, they each offered and accepted tiny gestures of peace. Finally, they sat down less than a metre apart and went to sleep. Just fifteen minutes earlier they had screamed what they were going to do to each other.

This got me thinking about how young people, especially boys, find it so necessary to square up to each other. No one wants to be the first to back down – that would be soft – and yet neither do they want to fight. It's all about projecting the right image. And all this from watching an encounter between two cats. Reflection brings about new learning from everyday experiences.

2. *Reflection brings about change*

We are often constrained by convention, trapped by routine and locked into doing things the way they have always been done. Whilst convention can bring reassurance, it can also restrict our ability to solve problems. History is littered with the bones of good organisations that didn't adapt to momentous changes. Youth work and ministry requires a high degree of change to remain relevant for successive generations of young people. What worked in your youth is not guaranteed to work today – so don't be hasty with the Motorhead or Bay City Roller records. Equally, what works for one group of young people often does not work for another – even though they are from the same town. If you are to remain relevant, you need to reflect on the challenges you face.

3. *Reflection brings about self-awareness*

It is also possible to overlook the complexity of human life, taking insufficient account of our personality and experiences and the impact we have on other people's personality and experiences. Your childhood experiences indirectly influence your approach to life today. Having a greater awareness of who you are, and what shapes your personality, enables you to forge effective relationships with others, including young people.

There are four stages to reflection,[2] starting with 'the experience' and identification of what happened. We are concerned to know the facts, such as names, places, times and chronology of events. From here we move on to 'reflection', where we begin to analyse how and why this happened and the feelings it generated. This involves digging beneath the surface and connecting seemingly separate data. Key questions to ask include:

● What effect did it have on you and others?
● How did it make you and others feel?
● Why did you and others act and react in this way?
● What other options were available to you and others?

This is followed by 'understanding' and the drawing of conclusions. As a result of reflecting on the experience,

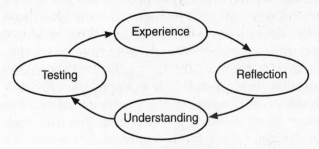

Kolb's Learning Circle

new learning is identified and theories constructed. Finally, these theories are examined in the 'testing' stage to see if they remain valid in the real world. The cycle is then repeated with new experiences, some of which are made in response to the learning that has been tested.

Reflection requires critical thinking. This is different from cynicism. Critical thinking is positive. It prompts enquiry and challenges convention in the belief that things can always change for the better. It is not afraid to ask awkward questions or to identify weaknesses as well as strengths, threats as well as opportunities. Youth work and ministry thrives on critical thinking. Cynicism, on the other hand, is negative. It curtails enquiry and mocks the possibility of change. This undermines youth work and ministry. Too little critical thinking and too much cynicism is a recipe for disaster.

Reflection rarely just happens. It is a discipline that has to be practised. Take a few minutes at the end of each session to discuss with your co-workers how it went and what, if any, action is required. It is good practice to record the key statistics and events in a logbook for future reference. This might include a register of people attending and the names of responsible youth workers on duty, a summary of the programme and a description of key incidents plus action taken or required.

Reflection is also developed through consistent participation in regular team meetings. This creates an opportunity for more in-depth reflection and critical thinking. Just occasionally, it is also worth spending an extended time together. For example, plan to attend Youthwork – the Conference, the weekend conference for volunteer youth workers. You may find that time spent together outside of the formal conference programme is almost as helpful as the sessions themselves.

To think about...
Think about something you have learnt as a result of reflecting on your practice. How do you ensure you continue to learn from your practice?

Character

The way you live your life matters. It speaks volumes about your beliefs and values. As a volunteer, you may only see the young people you serve for two of the 168 hours in a week. It is tempting to think that youth work and ministry is only concerned with what you do during this 0.8 per cent of the week. A fraction of an iceberg appears above the waterline, while its significant bulk is hidden and dangerous. Sailors ignore this at their peril. What you do and how you behave during the 99.2 per cent of the week you are not with your young people determines the authority you have during the short time you are with them. This is because your authority stems from who you are, not from your position or organisational context.

Those who observed Jesus were amazed because he taught as one who had real authority (Mt. 7:29; 9:6). Unlike the Pharisees, who maintained a façade of religious convention, Jesus made sure that his inner life and outward actions authenticated his message. He didn't just talk about forgiveness; he practised it. Even if he had never uttered a word about hospitality, his onlookers would have been in no doubt of its importance in his radical new kingdom agenda.

People model themselves on others all the time. They observe what they do and what the consequences are, and then adjust their behaviour accordingly. Like it or not, you are a role model for the young people you serve. They will model their lives according to the example you set. This means you have the power to influence them – both positively and negatively. Therefore you have a responsibility to consider your actions and lifestyle, striving through your example to point young people towards Christ. This was the Apostle Paul's ambition (1 Cor. 11:1; 2 Thes. 3:9). Only you will know the kind of issues that this highlights in your life.

Young people can be ruthless in spotting inconsistencies between words and deeds. If your actions and lifestyle are inconsistent with your message, you will be found out and your message will be undermined. This confuses young people. It is not enough to talk about the core values of voluntary participation, informal education, empowerment, equality of opportunity and incarnation (see Chapter One), they should be evident in the way you live your life and treat others. Think for a moment about your attitudes towards money, sex and power. To what extent can they be considered Christian?

Highlighting the importance of character doesn't mean that only perfect human beings need apply for 'extra-timer' positions. Like me, you will occasionally make mistakes. The good news is that we are not alone. The Apostle Paul was refreshingly honest about his own failings (Rom. 7:14–24). The challenge is to be aware of and honest about your shortcomings, whilst continually striving to be more Christ-like.

To think about...
What qualities and character traits do you believe are most important for those who serve young people and why? How do you deal with your own inconsistencies?

Spirituality

Whereas youth and community work is generally focussed on physical and social development, youth work and ministry gives greater recognition to the spiritual needs of young people. Volunteers and staff are therefore expected to be Christians who are motivated and empowered by their faith.

You are not just a volunteer youth worker. You are also a Christian. Just like everyone else, you need to know

God's love, grace and empowerment in your life. Youth work and ministry is not always easy. Sometimes you will feel ineffective or frustrated. Occasionally you may even want to give up and become a house group leader or join the choir – in fact, do anything other than youth work and ministry. That is when you need to know God's activity in your life. If it helps, by doing this you will model to young people what it means to be a follower of Christ – as God intended.

To think about…
In the midst of your busy life, how do you maintain your love for Christ? What keeps your faith active and growing?

You are not just a volunteer youth worker. You are also a minister of the gospel. This means, you are God's representative to the young people you serve. You are a channel of his blessing. You may even be the only one placed to offer this.

You will want to pray regularly for the young people you serve. The more you build positive relationships with them, the more specific your prayers can be. You will also be conscious of the spiritual example you are setting. The young people you serve will inevitably make judgments about the Christian faith based largely on what they see in you. For example, they are more likely to believe in the power of prayer if they see and hear how you pray. You cannot lead young people to where you have not been yourself.

Above all, young people need you to be spiritually real. Fortunately they don't require you to be a super saint who never misses daily prayer and Bible study (unless of course you are and don't). They may be reassured to know that you too sometimes face spiritual challenges or obstacles that don't disappear with a quick prayer. You should be as open and honest with the young people about your faith as you want them to be about theirs. To be a committed Christian is not to declare you have spiritually arrived (as if you could ever exhaust God's potential), but to know that there is always more to God than you have as yet experienced. It is a lifelong journey. You have come a long way, but mercifully have much further still to go.

Belonging

The church is often ridiculed, criticised and, worst of all, ignored. It's not difficult to see why. Too many of our worship services are dull, our buildings are decaying, and we are silent on the issues of the day. Even the most dynamic congregations have some faults. After all, you and I are involved.

The church is also the Bride of Christ (Eph. 5:22–27). Jesus loves the church enough to surrender his life for her. You should love what Christ loves – the church and your local congregation. Love does not continually ridicule, criticise or reject. Paul put it like this:

Love is patient.
  (*even when nothing ever seems to change from one year to the next*)
Love is kind.
  (*especially to Mrs Braithwaite, with the loose fitting dentures and hairy chin, who always moans about the young people*)
Love does not envy.
  (*even those who belong to a more appealing church just down the road*)
Love does not boast.
  (*despite knowing its ideas and skills could turn the congregation around*)
Love is not proud.
  (*when once again it is asked to serve the teas and coffees*)
Love is not rude.
  (*even when you are expected to close the youth group every time the choir needs an extra room for rehearsal*)

Love is not self-seeking.
  (*recognising that its preference isn't everyone else's*)
Love is not easily angered.
  (*even when young people are only ever mentioned in church meetings if there is damage to report*)
Love keeps no record of wrongs.
  (*not mentioning all the broken promises about creating a youth budget*)
Love does not delight in evil, but rejoices with the truth
You see, love always protects, always trusts, always hopes, always perseveres. Love never fails.

                                          Based on 1 Corinthians 13:4–8

You should be careful not to speak badly of the church in general or your own congregation. Remember, you share responsibility for it. It is better to talk of 'we' rather than 'they'. As difficult as this may be at times, you should show your love for the church – Christ's bride.

However, to love is also to seek the best. This means sometimes you will love the church enough to risk your reputation in order to identify and face up to some of her weaknesses. The challenge is to do this in a loving, constructive and affirming way. The church needs critical thinkers; not cynics.

It is important to model to young people how they can be agents for change. They need to see how you engage with, and challenge, those who see things differently. You should be an active participant in the life of your local congregation. Fortunately, this is not measured by the number of committees you belong to. But neither should you give up meeting with other Christians, as some are in the habit of doing (Heb. 10:25). You need to give and receive the encouragement and accountability that belonging to a local Christian community offers.

To think about...
When, if at all, do you find yourself having
to defend either the church at large or your
local congregation? On reflection, what
impression of the church do young people
derive from your example?

The next chapter, 'Developing outreach', looks at mission
and evangelism. This will enable you to grow your youth
work and ministry. But first let's recap on what we have
covered in this chapter.

Summary

- Reflection is the ability to step outside of a situation
  and see things differently. It is concerned not so much
  with what happens as how and why things happen.
- Critical thinking asks challenging questions and thinks
  the unimaginable because it believes things can always
  be improved.
- The way you live your life matters – it speaks volumes
  about your beliefs and values. Like it or not, you are
  a role model for the young people you serve with the
  power to influence them positively or negatively.
- Your own spirituality also matters. You need to know
  God's love, grace and empowerment in your life. Young
  people will make judgments about the Christian faith
  based, largely, on what they see in you.
- The church is the Bride of Christ. He loves the church
  enough to give up his life for her – and so should
  you.

Notes

1. Taken from the film *Antz* © 2002, DreamWorks Pictures.
2. Based on Kolb, D. (1984), *Experiential Learning*, Englewood Cliffs, NY: Prentice-Hall.

PART THREE

DEVELOPING

7

Developing outreach

The Good News

On a recent day off, my wife and I went out for lunch. We had looked forward to visiting this street café for some time, and were anticipating a time of quiet togetherness. We had just started to eat when the peace was shattered by some rowdy buskers. The guitar was missing a string, and the singers could only be described as musically challenged. Quite how the lady with the tambourine managed to miss the beat so consistently was beyond belief. They were, however, faithfully declaring the good news. Our noisy buskers were Christians, intent on proclaiming the gospel to everyone within shouting distance. But the louder they wailed, the further away they drove their listeners.

After a while there was a lull in the barrage. Calling them songs would be open to challenge under the Trade Descriptions Act. The 'buskers' looked apprehensively at each other and the passers-by until the signal was given for a final assault. A man stepped forward and began to shout. He delivered a bizarre version of the good news that denounced everyone with HIV and AIDS, the divorced and those struggling with alcohol dependence. Before long the catch-all 'original sin' was unleashed, with devastating effect; nobody could escape his attack. The good news turned out to be bad news. Not surprisingly, no one responded to his message. But the group seemed pleased that once again the word had gone forth and, God willing, would not return void. I was left wanting to stand up and apologise to my fellow diners for what had been inflicted on them in the name of Christ.

Christians talk a lot about the good news, often without stopping to consider how good it really is. Youth work and ministry gives young people an opportunity to experience the good news of God's kingdom for themselves. You will be most effective if you are convinced that God's kingdom actually works, so we begin our look at developing outreach by considering God's open and inclusive kingdom.[1]

God is open and inclusive

Contrary to popular misconception, God is open and inclusive. He appears to be more generous and less judgmental than many of his representatives on earth. It is we who are sometimes quick to judge. This is evident from Christ's life and witness. Where the Pharisees excluded all those who didn't conform to their narrow understanding of religious acceptability, Jesus was inclusive. He condemned their distorted view of God (Mt. 16:5–12; 21:12–16; Lk. 11:37–54) and demonstrated that the kingdom of heaven is for everyone.

To describe Christ's agenda as 'good news' seems almost an understatement. It was totally fantastic news for everybody the Pharisees had labelled worthless. These included the least respected in society (e.g. shepherds

– Lk. 2:8–18); those infected with socially unacceptable diseases (e.g. lepers – Lk. 5:12–14); the physically
imperfect (e.g. the disabled – Mk. 8:22–26; Lk. 5:17–25);
those of the wrong gender (e.g. women – Lk. 10:38–42);
those who were too young (e.g. children – Lk. 18:15–17);
those working in dodgy professions (e.g. tax collectors
– Lk. 5:27–32; 19:1–10); the psychiatrically oppressed (Lk.
4:33–36; 9:37–42); law breakers (e.g. revolutionaries – Mt.
10:4); foreigners (e.g. Samaritans – Lk. 10:25–37); and the
promiscuous (Lk. 7:36–50). The list was almost endless.
Through his actions, Jesus convinced these people that
God was very open towards them.

Perhaps unsurprisingly, Jesus encountered stiff oppo-
sition from the first-century Jewish authorities. They
considered him to be a threat, and they were right – he
was. Jesus challenged their mistaken belief in their own
importance and privileged position. God had not called
them to be bouncers, pushing crowds of would-be wor-
shippers away from the doors of heaven. He wanted them
to be hospitable party planners, bringing joy to people
who normally felt left out. God blessed Israel so that she
would bless the whole world (Gen. 12:1–3). God's radical
kingdom was always intended to be for the Gentiles as
well as the Jews. The Pharisees had accepted the blessing,
but not the responsibility.

Following Christ's example, youth work and ministry
should also be open and inclusive. It is for the 'messed
up' as much as for the 'sorted'. It should bless all young
people and communities, and not be a private activity for
the social élite. A tragically large amount of youth work
and ministry in Britain today engages only with socially,
economically and politically advantaged young people,
many of them born into a church-attending tradition. For
these youngsters, youth work and ministry is a spiritual
enclave designed to shield them from 'undesirables'.[2] Not

nearly enough time or energy is invested in reaching out to socially disadvantaged or excluded young people.

To what extent does your practice reach out to, and engage with, those young people who do not conform to the pattern?

To think about...
How does this vision of good news compare with some expressions of Christian belief today? To what extent does your youth work and ministry demonstrate good news to the young people in your community?

You are a partner with God

Over the course of two thousand years Christianity has grown from a dozen disciples into the world's largest religious movement. Over two billion people claim it as their own. The key to this phenomenal growth is the missionary zeal of believers. After all, the good news of God's kingdom is just too good to keep hidden from people.

Youth work and ministry is primarily about mission. It's about enabling young people to experience God's openness and inclusiveness for themselves so they can claim the life that God always intended for them (Jn. 10:10). Through mission, we join in with God's activity in the world, continuing the work that Christ began (Jn. 14:12). This means copying all that Christ did, said and stood for. Jesus fed the hungry, socialised with the lonely and healed the sick as much as he taught religious education. Mission is therefore broad, encompassing social, political and spiritual outcomes. Evangelism is a narrower specialist activity within mission and is concerned with proclamation and calling people to respond to the good news about God's inclusive kingdom.

Youth work and ministry must therefore encompass some form of outreach. The question is, what form should this take?

Values-based outreach

Some Christians believe 'the end justifies the means', so it is OK to do anything that results in someone receiving eternal salvation. After all, isn't the prospect of eternal damnation far worse? This is the same argument used by police officers when they go through a red traffic light – it is wrong, but if it enables a more efficient response the greater good is served. Others maintain that 'the means validate the end'. Who wants to spend eternity in a place they'd never accept without being tricked? Values help inform decisions. The values of youth work and ministry result in outreach that is both ethical and effective.

Ethical outreach

Chapter One identified the five values of youth work and ministry as being voluntary participation, informal education, empowerment, equality of opportunity, and incarnation. These prevent youth work and ministry from adopting unethical means. For example, the value of voluntary participation requires a young person to make a free and informed decision to become involved – nothing less. I believe it is unethical to invite young people to attend a free gig without telling them it is organised by a church and halfway through will have a presentation about Christianity. To turn off the music and launch into a 30-minute, emotionally charged, hard-sell presentation without warning people seems wrong. This is a classic cult trick. It is not what Christ needs his church to do.

In the Old Testament, Abram and Sarai were promised children but Sarai didn't conceive (Gen. 12:1–3; 15:1–6). Fearing that God was either distracted or incapable of fulfilling his promise, they decided to give him a hand. Sarai chose her servant to be a surrogate mother (Gen. 16:1–4). Abram and Sarai thought they were assisting God in his plan, but showed a basic lack of faith in God. In the same way, those engaged in youth work and ministry should not resort to unethical means to 'assist' God. It completely misses the point of the good news and suggests a basic lack of faith in God.

To think about...
Is it ever right to ignore the rights of young people for the sake of a `higher good`? If so, when and why? To what extent is the outreach within your youth work and ministry ethical?

Relational outreach

God is seeking a relationship with us, his creation, and he is prepared to take risks to enable us to reciprocate. Through the incarnation he demonstrated the extent of his love. John's Gospel begins with a description of the Word (Jn. 1:1–18), which is not a set of doctrinal statements or sermons but God the Son. The Word had a pulse, feelings and moved into our neighbourhood. Youth work and ministry, with its value of incarnation, enables young people to establish a relationship with the Word, to know God for themselves. If the young people you seek to serve are to engage with God, you first need to engage with them.

There is no substitute for relationships. Outreach is not about providing a funky expression of faith, delivering a 'hard sell' presentation or providing a watertight argument. It is about one human being engaging with another so that they can engage with God.

Outreach programmes and techniques can be useful, but only as a supplement to the relationship between the young person and youth worker. Never as a replacement. For this reason, outreach draws upon all the values and skills of youth work and ministry covered so far. Because of the value of informal education, outreach starts where young people are at – emotionally and intellectually. There is little point giving answers to questions that aren't being asked and staying silent on the issues they are struggling with. This is what makes Christianity appear utterly irrelevant to many people. It is far better to engage in conversation with youngsters as this enables you both to ask questions and offer answers.

To think about…
What does your outreach rely upon more: programmes or relationships? How does informal education feature in your outreach?

Directing outreach

There are two broad approaches to mission: 'inside out' and 'outside in'.[3] One is not necessarily better but neither is capable of reaching all young people. Some groups pursue just one approach. Others operate the two in parallel. So what are they?

Inside out

Believing that young people have a responsibility and are best placed to reach out to their peers, the 'inside out' model starts from the inside and works outwards in a ripple effect. It begins with a core group of young people who are committed to the Christian ethos of the group. They are empowered to be effective in reaching out to their peers through a combination of inspirational teaching and training, plus the provision of credible events to which they can invite their friends. The group grows as the core members invite their non-member friends to join.

Effectiveness of the 'inside out' model depends on:

● A quorum of young people being available to form the core
● Core members having friends outside of their group and faith
● Core members being sufficiently motivated and capable of talking openly about their group and faith
● The provision of suitable activities to which core members can invite their friends

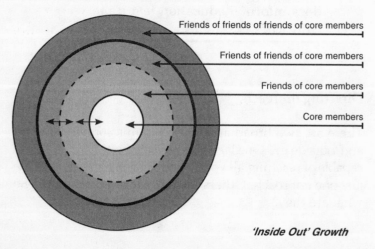

Friends of friends of friends of core members

Friends of friends of core members

Friends of core members

Core members

'Inside Out' Growth

Willow Creek Community Church[4] near Chicago, USA, has grown from a youth group into a church of over 20,000 people using an 'inside out' model. Their 'seven steps' strategy is based on:

1. *Authentic friendship*
   Core members are encouraged to develop strong friend-ships with those outside, as well as in, the group.

2. *Verbal witness*
   Core members are enabled to speak about their belong-ing and beliefs with their friends.

3. *Seeker event*
   Core members are encouraged to invite their friends to group events that are specifically designed for non-members.

4. *Spiritual challenge*
   Non-members are given opportunity for response to presentations of the Christian faith.

5. *Integration into the church*
   New believers are encouraged to participate in worship services.

6. *Small group*
   New believers are invited to join a small group.

7. *Ownership*
   New believers become core members when they start to develop strong friendships with those outside, as well as in, the group and speak about their newly acquired belonging and beliefs.

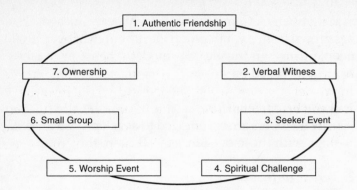

Willow Creek's 'Seven Steps'

The seven steps can be applied in churches big and small and together form a continuous growth cycle.

The 'inside out' approach has both advantages and disadvantages.

Positively, it places great emphasis on the empowerment of core group members, who are enabled to reach their full God-given potential. It values friendship and ensures a strong mission focus is maintained. It also produces slow, steady and sustainable growth as young people gradually invite those within their friendship circle to join them. This, however, gives hint to some of its weaknesses.

Negatively, 'like attracts like'. What of those young people who are outside the friendship circles of group members? This approach does not generally cross socio-economic divides or promote diversity. It can pressurise young core members to achieve results. There is always a risk that those outside of the group may not be impressed if they observe double standards in core members. This is sufficient justification for looking at the alternative approach.

Outside in

Recognising that some young people are beyond the reach of most core members in church youth groups, the 'outside in' model starts from the outside and works inwards. It makes a beeline for those culturally and socially furthest from the church group, who may be on the streets, in the park or at a community project. A church-sponsored open youth club with few core members may exhibit 'outside in' characteristics.

It isn't the youth workers who determine the rules and social conventions but the young people. They also decide what happens. An 'outside in' youth worker is a guest who seeks to understand and build rapport with the individuals and groups of young people. There is no knowing how an 'outside in' youth worker will be received, just as young people are equally uncertain how they will be received by an 'inside out' youth group. It is only after the youth worker has established their credibility that opportunities arise to discuss matters of faith and belief. But then it is always a two-way dialogue, never a one-way monologue.

'Outside in' youth work and ministry is missionary-like in its incarnational approach to engaging with hard-to-reach groups of young people. Just as Christ left the security of heaven to enter the world powerless and vulnerable (Phil. 2:5–11), so youth workers leave the security of church youth groups to enter the subcultures of young people powerless and vulnerable.

As relationships are formed, some young people will show signs of wanting to explore issues of belonging and belief. Instead of directing them to the 'inside out' church youth group, the 'outside in' model enables streetwise young people to form a new core. If the church is perceived as a building and an order of service, then the new 'outside in' core will remain beyond its covering. However, an alternative is to recognise the new core as stretching the reach of the church into new places and communities.

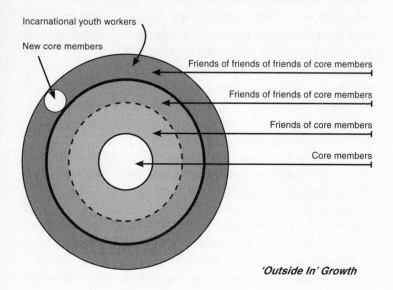

'Outside In' Growth

Just as with 'inside out', there are advantages and disadvantages to the 'outside in' approach.

Positively, it has a strong incarnational focus, going to where young people are. It is therefore inclusive of the groups of young people beyond the church's traditional reach. It too values peer groups and creates opportunities for Christian spirituality to be made relevant to more subcultures.

Negatively, youth workers can sometimes feel vulnerable and isolated as they explore beyond the safety of the church. Once relationships are established, there are then complex issues of integration to resolve. New street-level core groups are sometimes labelled second best to traditional 'inside out' groups.

Both 'inside out' and 'outside in' approaches have strengths and weaknesses. The question is, which approach do you favour? Before deciding, it is worth remembering that the vast majority of youth work and ministry is currently 'inside out'. This is primarily due to its ease and its popularity with church-attending parents. If you fall in step, what will become of those youngsters beyond the reach of your group or church? Some need to become 'outside in'.

Conversation and conversion

It is crucial for youth workers to adopt a natural approach in relating to young people. Even the busiest person has at least some interests or hobbies. Most aren't too difficult or embarrassing to talk about with friends. That's what friendship is all about. The key is conversation and relationship. The challenge is to debunk the dreaded 'witnessing' that makes Christianity a hard-to-mention topic.

Christians sometimes feel under great pressure to 'convert' people. The harder they try, the more off-putting they become. Just think how you react to pushy sales staff who try to sell you things you neither need nor want.

Through conversation we challenge others and are, in turn, challenged by them. Some approaches to evangelism are unnatural and conversation stoppers. The challenge is to win people, not arguments. Pushy evangelism tries to force people into making decisions they are not ready to make. To protect themselves, undecided people will say 'no' and then, for the first time in their life, they become non-Christians. Ironically, it is often Christians who turn people into non-Christians. A person-centred approach – actively listening to where people are at – ensures an opportunity for response is given at just the right moment. A good indicator is people asking what they should do to connect with God (Acts 2:37). Asking this question means they are probably well on their spiritual journey.

It is equally important to adopt an enabling approach. Youth work and ministry can equip Christian young people to talk openly about their beliefs. Youth for Christ (YfC) have developed an approach they call 'three story evangelism' that is affirming and practical (see the Resource Directory at the back of this book).

The following tips will help you to equip your young people to share their beliefs with others.

1. Set an example for young people to follow.

If they are to talk about their belonging and beliefs with their friends, then they need to know and see how you do this with yours.

2. Build up their confidence and openness.

Help them to be natural by being natural yourself. Avoid pressuring young people or instructing them in sales techniques. They are not a resource to be exploited; they are people to be loved. Consistently encourage young people, whether they have a go or not. Don't use praise to reward success, and rejection or avoidance to punish failure.

3. Provide credible opportunities for them to invite their friends.

Young people often need to belong before they can believe. Providing cringe-free, relaxed opportunities to include others can help the group to experience growth from its fringe.

4. *Promote respect for those of other traditions and beliefs.*
   Avoid producing well-drilled and argumentative believers, armed with facts and apologetics. Inclusive and loving believers best demonstrate God's inclusive kingdom.

In the next chapter, 'Developing spirituality', we shall look at ways to promote young people's spirituality and Christian discipleship. This will enable you to create a positive and inspiring environment that encourages young people to pursue spiritual growth. First, here's a reminder of what has been included in this chapter.

Summary

- The good news is that God's radical kingdom is open and inclusive of all people, including those who are disadvantaged and socially excluded.
- Christians are called to be partners with God in reaching out to those beyond the reach of the church.
- The values of youth work and ministry prevent the use of unethical methods of evangelism. Positively, they enable effective, relational outreach.
- The 'inside out' approach empowers core young people to reach out to their peers, whereas the 'outside in' approach leaves the security of the local congregation and goes to where hard-to-reach young people are.
- Outreach relies as much on conversation as conversion. Talking about belonging and beliefs should be natural and honest.

NOTES

1. This theme is developed further in my book *Joined-Up: An Introduction to Youth Work and Ministry* (Authentic, 2003) and by Steve Chalke in *The Lost Message of Jesus* (Hodder, 2004).
2. Pete Ward, in *Growing Up Evangelical* (SPCK, 1996), argues that much evangelical youth work is now motivated not by mission but by a desire to create safety for young people of church-attending families.
3. For a more detailed explanation see Mike Breen's *Outside In: reaching un-churched young people today* (Scripture Union, 1993) or Pete Ward's *Youthwork and the Mission of God* (SPCK, 1997).
4. For further information about Willow Creek Community Church, and their Sonlight (Junior High), Student Impact (Senior High) and Axis (18 to 20-somethings) programmes visit www.willowcreek.org or read Bo Bosher's *Student Ministry for the 21st Century* (Zondervan/Willow Creek Resources, 1997).

8

Developing spirituality

The Marx Brothers were brought up on 93rd Street in the Bronx, New York City. The family was poor, and it was Chico alone who got piano lessons. With five children, they couldn't really afford even this. But Minnie, their resourceful mother, scraped together enough money each week to hire the cheapest piano teacher in all of New York City. So Chico started piano lessons. He was quick to learn but rarely practised.

After months of playing with the right hand, Chico eventually plucked up courage and asked his teacher what he was meant to do with the other hand. To his surprise, the teacher told him to fake it because not even world famous concert pianists played with their left hand. They all played just with their right hand. Minnie had hired the only piano teacher in the city who didn't know how to play the piano with both hands.

Chico grew up to be the fastest one-handed piano player in all of New York. Being enterprising, he got jobs in nickelodeons accompanying the silent movies. With lightning speed, and just one hand, he could maintain the pace of an express train hurtling down a mountainside with failed brakes and an over-excited projectionist – and all because of what he had learnt from a one-hand-playing piano teacher.

Teachers, it seems, have an enormous impact on their pupils. As an extra-timer you are well placed to support a young person's spiritual development. This chapter is all about how to develop spirituality and discipleship in young people. Once again, greater emphasis will be given to your own example and personality, over and above that of structured programmes. But first we need to clarify what is meant by spirituality and discipleship.

Spirituality and discipleship

Spirituality has become fashionable. Some people won't start the day without yoga, whilst others couldn't move a table without feng shui. Everything from eastern mysticism and appreciation of Islamic culture to love of the environment is now called 'spiritual'. In its lowest form, it has become whatever moves you.

Christianity affirms the value of spirituality. It is the search for meaning beyond the physical realm, a thirst for reality that is unquenched by water alone (Jn. 4:13–14). Young people do not become spiritual when they decide to follow Christ. We are all born spiritual. It is as if God breathes this into every newborn baby (Gen. 2:7). Youth work and ministry provides a safe and supportive environment in which young people can discover their spiritual nature. Christians maintain this is best satisfied in Christ. As an extra-timer, your challenge is not to stop young people looking in the wrong places but to promote genuine spiritual enquiry. Jesus promised: "Everyone who asks receives; he who seeks finds; and to him who knocks, the door will be opened." (Mt. 7:8)

Discipleship is a process of transformation by which one person is changed through interaction with another.

In the first century, people became disciples of the rabbi they wanted to be like. The apostle Paul wrote:

> "Therefore, I urge you, brothers, in view of God's mercy, to offer your bodies as living sacrifices, holy and pleasing to God – this is your spiritual act of worship. Do not conform any longer to the pattern of this world, but be transformed by the renewing of your mind." (Rom. 12:1–2)

To be transformed is to be changed from one state to another. Metamorphosis (which comes from the Greek word for transformation) is the process by which, for example, a caterpillar is transformed into a butterfly. Youth work and ministry offers young people the possibility of transformation into a new way of living. They grasp this by copying what they see in you.

Authentic Christian discipleship is always challenging. It is living according to God's agenda, not our own. Jesus said: "If anyone would come after me, he must deny himself and take up his cross and follow me. For whoever wants to save his life will lose it, but whoever loses his life for me will find it." (Mt. 16:24–25) Grace may be free but discipleship is never cheap. Our superficial 'entertain me' world looks for discipleship at discounted rates. We are encouraged to embrace what is enjoyable and discard what is dull or demanding. Youth work and ministry must enable young people to embrace authentic Christian discipleship, with all its privileges and responsibilities.

To think about...
To what extent are the young people you serve aware of their spiritual nature and how are they currently seeking to quench its thirst? How do you stimulate young people's spiritual enquiry?

Making disciples

Youth work and ministry seeks to fulfil Jesus' command to "go and make disciples of all nations," (Mt. 28:19). Making disciples is both a privilege and a responsibility. As a volunteer, you have the capacity to influence the young people you serve; both positively and negatively. Young people will learn more from your example than from your words. Chico's piano playing potential was restricted by his piano teacher's own abilities. You should consider what you are discipling young people into. Your own spirituality and Christian discipleship are of importance. What are you modelling to the young people you serve?

Discipling is not about telling young people how to live their lives or making decisions for them. Rather, it is about empowering them to take responsibility for themselves. It should be enabling, never controlling as this, if unchecked, can lead to religious abuse. It can be hard enough to control your own life, never mind trying to control others.

Knowing that others appreciate you can be very satisfying. You should take great care not to create, however unintentionally, a provider-client trap in which young people develop an unhealthy dependency on you. This can occur through a lack of reflection or personal security. How do you derive security?

It can be painful to watch young people struggle with life issues, but you should not be quick to intervene or solve their problems – even when you can. To do so risks spoiling their opportunity for learning and growth. Paul tells us that trials have a purpose.

"These [trials] have come so that your faith – of greater worth than gold, which perishes even though refined by fire

– may be proved genuine and may result in praise, glory and honour when Jesus Christ is revealed." (1 Pet. 1:7)

Sometimes it is necessary to offer young people support and encouragement, still taking care not to wrestle their problems away from them. You should not see yourself as a young person's saviour. They already have one who is more than capable of meeting their deepest need.

Your discipling must also be accessible. Making disciples is not just about religious instruction. If it were, it could be completed in a short course delivered by computers! It is about sharing your life with others, letting them see how you deal with routine, as well as rare, situations. This requires a degree of availability outside of formal group sessions. Meals and other social occasions can be significant.

Being accessible to young people must be balanced against the need for safe practice. This means always ensuring you invite groups of young people, not individuals; always meeting in a public space such as a café, not in a private setting such as your house; always informing co-workers about who, when and where you are meeting; and being careful not to get too familiar with young people, such that an outsider could interpret your actions as being grooming a minor for later sexual gratification. Particular thought should be given to the content of emails and text messages.

To think about...
How do you decide when it is appropriate to intervene with young people who are struggling? How do you balance availability to young people with your other time commitments and safe practice requirements?

Spiritual disciplines

For many evangelicals, the evidence of discipleship is to be found in daily Bible readings and prayer. While certainly useful, such disciplines are not the 'be all and end all' of discipleship. There are many more spiritual disciplines, including fasting, simplicity, solitude and service.[1] It is also important to remember that discipleship is the process of growing into the likeness of Christ. It is a 24-7 relationship, not a twenty-minute duty before bed. That said, let's look at ways of enabling young people to develop the spiritual disciplines of worship, Bible reading and giving.

Worship

Worship is the spiritual discipline many Christian young people appear most enthusiastic about, but what is worship and how can it be nurtured?

The Anglo-Saxon root of the word is 'worth-ship', meaning worship is to attribute value to something. A Christian worships when they recognise God's worth. It is more an attitude than an activity. It does not happen in a service and end with the closing benediction, but goes on at all times in all places.

1. Participative

Worship should be participative. In the Old Testament, the priests alone were permitted to worship in the holy of holies; everyone else was confined to the sidelines. Jesus replaced the exclusive temple system with a new access all areas policy (Mt. 27:51; Heb. 8:1–2; 10:19–20). Now everyone is granted equal opportunity to worship God in spirit and truth (Jn. 4:24). Jesus didn't do away with the priestly system, he simply made all believers priests (1 Pet. 2:9) and this includes young people.

Some churches have replaced one-man ministry with one-band ministry. It is sometimes musically more dynamic, but no more participative – many people are still rendered spectators. Because youth work and ministry values voluntary participation, we ensure that everyone who wants to has an active part in worship. This requires more creative expressions of worship.

2. Creative

Worship should be a creative reflection of God's character. Music has always featured in Judeo-Christian worship (Ex. 15:1–18,20–21; Ps. 96:1–2; 150:1–6; Lk. 1:46–55; 1 Cor. 14:26). Over time the musical style and lyrics have changed, but their role has not. There is more to worship than singing songs, however. Many young people have been brought up on choruses and find this hard to comprehend, but singing can be a hindrance for those who are self-conscious about their developing voices and identity formation. Liturgy, Bible readings and prayers can be fused with dance music, audio-visual experiences, spray-painting and poetry, among other things, to create a participative worship experience.

God designed us with five senses – sight, sound, taste, touch and smell. All of them can be stimulated in worship. Communion is perhaps the best example of sense-appealing worship because it involves all the senses, though this has been mysteriously reduced to an uncreative and senseless experience in many 'low' churches today.

3. Challenging

Worship should challenge the status quo. Youth work and ministry enables young people to express God's worth in culturally relevant ways. The charismatic movement was born during the 1960s hippie revolution. While Simon and Garfunkel sang of love and peace, young Christians were introducing greater informality to Christian worship. Mirroring elements of popular youth culture, they replaced church organs with guitars and drums and created the melodic folk songs that have become typical of mainstream evangelical worship today. The church tends to resist change before eventually relenting. Within twenty years the new way becomes the tradition that another generation of young people has to challenge. As an extra-timer, your role is to empower young people to challenge the status quo in your church and enable them to find new creative expressions of worship.

4. *Community based*
Worship should include corporate responses to God. Some postmodern expressions of worship appear to adopt the mantra 'me, myself and I'. Lyrics are written in the first person, and are all about me and my response to God. There is surprisingly little emphasis on God and his response to us. What's good about this is that it has fostered a new intimacy in worship, but there is a risk and its name is immaturity. For the first few years of life, we mistakenly believe the world revolves around us. When a baby cries, people come running. It is a shock to realise we are not the centre of the universe and that we share this world with others.

Youth work and ministry should enable young people to express their membership of the body of Christ. They are not alone. Furthermore, it should enable them to focus more on God's character, and less on their own flawed existence. It is more about proclaiming God's unchanging goodness than having a changeable devotion to him. Encourage your young people to write songs with lyrics that enable their group to make a shared response towards God.

To think about...
To what extent are young people able to participate in worship in your practice? What creative expressions of worship do, or could, your young people use? How do young people challenge the status quo in your church?

Bible reading

In complete or partial form, the Bible has been translated into 2,303 languages. It remains the best selling book of all time. Most Western Christians own numerous copies and new versions are being developed all the time. The choice can be baffling. Yet many young people find reading the Bible harder than prayer or worship. Its size and complexity can be intimidating. How, they ask, can a book written thousands of years ago about life on another continent be relevant for them today? Youth work and ministry, with its commitment to informal education and empowerment, finds creative and inspiring ways to help young people appreciate the Bible. Use these tips to develop your young people's use of the Bible

1. Know your young people

The approach you adopt will, in part, be dependent on the young people you serve. Those whose first language isn't English or who struggle with literacy will need a far more visual and narrative approach. For example, make good use of story telling of Bible events, role-play, drama, art, Bible videos and conversation. You should only ever ask people to read in public if you know they are capable of doing it. If in doubt, ask for volunteers.

Make sure you stock a translation that is easier to read. Some academically able young people will need a more challenging approach.

2. *Use the Bible to teach*

'Give a hungry person a fish and he'll eat for a day; give him a fishing net and he'll eat for a lifetime.' This is a classic world development principle. But it also applies to use of the Bible. Tell a young person a story and they'll be spiritually fed for a day; show them how to read the Bible and they'll be fed for a lifetime. It is not enough to talk about biblical themes; young people need to see where they originate from and to read the Bible for themselves. Talking about God's generosity towards people is OK; telling the story of the Prodigal Son is better. But showing young people how to find and understand Luke's account (Lk. 15:11–32) is better still. A fistful of funny stories and a spiritual punch line do not constitute Bible teaching.

3. *Teach for a response*

Jesus instructed his followers to teach people to "obey everything I have commanded you." (Mt. 28:20) Your task is not to drill young people in Bible trivia, but to help them bring about transformation in their lives by putting into practice what they learn. You should enable young people to determine their own responses to what they read in the Bible.

4. *Practise informal education*

Teaching the Bible need not be formal. In fact, Jesus characteristically used informal education methods such as conversation, storytelling, questions and answers, experiential learning-on-the-job and demonstrations of the miraculous. Some of the most inspired and life-changing teaching can arise from unplanned conversations. Make reference to the Bible in your conversations with young people.

5. *Invest yourself*

Think back to your teachers at school. You will have fond memories of some, and not of others. You should invest your own personality into your teaching and informal education. Your experiences, knowledge and personality can transform a session into a memorable and life-changing moment. Choose to invest energy into your sessions, especially when feeling tired. Remember; no matter how lively you feel, you will always come across as being less lively.

To think about...
Think through how you might use the account of the wise and foolish builders (Lk. 6:46–49) with the young people you serve. Write down key themes, possible teaching methods, points to consider etc.

Giving

Charities are getting ever more sophisticated in their fundraising techniques. Some entice young people with free days out, even holidays, in return for their involvement in sponsored events. The message given to young people is: 'Come and have an amazing experience for free – your friends and family will pay for it.' Consequently, the spiritual discipline of giving is being replaced by the technique of fleecing.

Giving is an important Christian habit. It is done in private, never for show (Mt. 6:1–4), and is a reflection of

God's generosity (Jn. 3:16). Through giving we renounce our love of money (Mt. 6:24; 1 Tim. 6:10) and renew our trust in God. In short, giving matters. A young person once asked me if our church would sponsor him to complete a parachute jump. He was raising money for a well-known charity. Knowing he had a high disposable income from a part-time job, I challenged him to give his own money to the cause. To help him, I agreed to match his giving pound for pound. Unfortunately, he never asked me for a penny. I would have been delighted if he had demanded a £100, but he had not learnt the art of giving.

Youth work and ministry should not shy away from challenging young people about their giving. Of course, how much they give, and to what cause, is strictly their decision. It is easier to develop the habit of giving when young. How do you enable young people to give and what example do you provide?

And still we haven't mentioned the spiritual disciplines of joy, simplicity, solitude, service and fasting among others. Your role as an extra-timer is to create an environment that inspires young people to discover their God-given spiritual capacity and ultimately become more Christ-like.

In the next chapter, 'Developing programmes', we will look at ways to develop healthy, balanced programmes and creative sessions. This will help you to decide what should be included and how to generate imaginative ideas. First, once again, we must review the content of this chapter.

Summary

- Spirituality is a search for reality beyond the physical realm. Youth work and ministry enables young people to discover their God-given spiritual capacity.

- Discipleship is a process of transformation whereby people become more Christ-like. Authentic Christian discipleship challenges the 'entertain me' culture of today.
- Making disciples is a key part of youth work and ministry. Discipling requires you to have a life worth living and be available to young people. It must be empowering, never controlling.
- Developing young people's worship requires you to be participative, creative, challenging and community-based.
- Developing young people's use of the Bible requires you to know your young people, use the Bible to teach, teach for a response, practise informal education and invest yourself.
- Young people can develop the spiritual discipline of giving.

NOTES

1. For a challenging introduction to spiritual disciplines read Richard Foster's *Celebration of Discipline* (Hodder & Stoughton, 1989)

9

Developing programmes

The youth team had spent months developing a new weekly programme for 11–14-year-olds. We had listened to their views and communicated with their parents. We had looked at a variety of resource packages and received specialist training. Confidence was high. No longer were we going to be seen as an extension of the children's ministry.

To mark the beginning of this new adventure, we kicked off with a truly hot session. The music was loud, the video screen full of crazy images and the smoke machine and lighting rig full on – it was an incredible atmosphere.

At the end of the session, I proudly strutted around fishing for positive feedback – and the occasional embarrassingly affirmative comment.

Certainly the first few young people I spoke to were impressed. I should have stopped while I was winning, but I couldn't resist asking everyone. I was like a pop star with a craving for adulation. The next young person I approached just shrugged his shoulders. Puzzled that he wasn't filled with enthusiasm and overflowing with praise, I enquired why he seemed so down.

His response shocked me.

'Why don't we ever go bird watching? It's always games,

videos and loud music,' he complained. 'We never go bird watching!'

My bubble was truly burst that night and I have never forgotten his comment.

Sometimes we assume we know what young people want. We mistakenly assume that all young people are the same and will therefore all like the same things. That is simply not the case. Our task as 'extra-time' youth workers is to devise programmes and sessions that are tailored to the unique needs of the individuals and groups we work with.

Sometimes we risk over-complicating things. We look for complex theories when a dose of old-fashioned common sense would suffice. This chapter relies heavily upon common sense and demonstrates that developing a programme and planning a session are not 'rocket science'. Use these simple tips to transform your youth work and ministry.

Planning a programme

Aims and goals

To start with, it is imperative that you have a clear aim. Aim at nothing and you're likely to hit it. You cannot plan a programme until you know what you want to achieve. By the middle of the term, start to think about what you want to achieve in the next term. Discuss this with your co-workers and, if applicable, the person responsible for co-ordinating youth work and ministry in your church. Pray and ask God to lead your deliberations.

Try to limit your aims to just one or two each term. Any more and you'll miss them all. Don't worry if your aims seem fairly broad. A few examples are:

- integrate recently joined members into the group
- create opportunities for members to invite their non-member friends to group activities
- prepare members for the summer community project
- start an Alpha for Youth course by the end of the term.

You may want to develop your aim(s) into SMART goals – Simple, Measurable, Achievable, Realistic, and Time-specific. SMART goals prevent you from being over-ambitious. They also congratulate you when they are achieved. Your SMART goals should be a response to a genuine need and serve as a statement of faith. With the aim and goals agreed, it is then possible to start planning your programme.

To think about...
What are the current aims of your youth work and ministry? What SMART targets should you aim for?

Young people's involvement

It is crucial that you involve young people in the programme. Voluntary participation is concerned as much with the quality of young people's involvement in the activities and decision-making as with their freedom to attend or not. Likewise, empowerment seeks opportunities for young people to assume control of their own lives. Both these values serve as reminders that young people must be involved in the group's decision-making and planning. Small youth groups are able to achieve this through informal means involving all members. Larger groups may need to consider adopting more formal mechanisms, such as an elected Youth Council. Young people's participation in the decision-making process is as much part of their development as any other activity, and helps to develop leadership skills.

To think about...
To what extent do young people participate in the decision-making and development of their youth work and ministry programme? What opportunities exist to increase their involvement to ensure the programme remains relevant to their needs?

Providing a balanced programme

Eating a balanced diet is key to healthy living. Feast only on burgers and fries, never on fresh fruit and vegetables, and you will suffer. Similarly, a balanced programme is key to developing a healthy, spiritually vibrant group. Youth work and ministry seeks to help young people develop physically, socially, emotionally, morally and spiritually. These basic developmental needs are common to all people, of all ages and cultures. You may find it helpful to use them as an aid to your programme planning. A multitude of activities and themes can be listed under them. For example:

Physical	Social	Emotional	Moral	Spiritual
Sports coaching	Meals	Sexual health education	Racism	Small/cell group
Competitions	Trips	Self-image	Crime	Bible study
Team games	Theme nights	Victim support	Violence	Worship service
Dance workshop	Make up/beauty treatments	Eating disorders	Sexism	Prayer group
Challenges	Parties	Drug education	Politics	Art of Connecting course
Outdoor pursuits	Residentials	Family	Justice	Evangelism
Weight training	Beach	Friendship	Media	Baptism/confirmation
Health education	Camping	Anger management	Consumerism	Alpha for Youth Course
Service project	Youth exchanges	Bullying support	Globalization	Communion
Ice skating	Games	Fears/anxiety	World debt	Festivals

In consultation with co-workers, young people, parents or guardians, and church leaders, decide to what extent each of these five developmental needs should feature as part of your provision. You will be unable to meet all needs, so focus on those that are not met as effectively elsewhere. You may decide the group should have a bias towards young people's spiritual development. If so, try splitting this into sub-aims such as God-focused, church-focused, world-focused, and me-focused. Again, a multitude of themes can be listed under these. For example:

God-focused

- Heaven
- Existence of God
- Prayer
- Worship
- Grace
- Fasting
- Angels

Me-focused

- Self-worth and image
- Sex and sexuality
- Sin and forgiveness
- Family and friendship
- Life and death
- Anxiety and fear
- Hopes and ambitions

World-focused

- Social concern
- Evangelism
- Justice
- The creation and the environment
- Kingdom of God
- Peace
- World mission

Church-focused

- Body of Christ and belonging
- Fellowship and community
- Leadership and authority
- Baptism/confirmation and communion
- Spiritual gifts
- Authority
- Servanthood

To think about...

What does your programme currently feature most and least? To what extent do you believe it offers young people a balanced diet? What, if any, adjustments need to be made?

Planning ahead

The difference between hitting aims and missing them is often planning. Things don't just fall into place by chance. In addition to prayer, it usually requires detailed planning. Unfortunately, youth workers are not known for their planning skills. Many find youth work and ministry stressful – not due to the demands of young people but because of their lack of planning and preparation. It's Thursday and Friday's a comin', they cry as they search frantically through back copies of *Youthwork Magazine*.

Develop the habit of thinking you are too busy not to plan. Planning ahead will alleviate stress and save you time and money. It will also aid you in communication, ensuring no one misses out on what you plan. Working as part of a team allows you to play to each other's strengths. Who likes getting into the detail of plans? The purpose of planning is to ensure you have the right people and resources in place at the right time. Only then will you be able to achieve agreed tasks. Who needs to know what, and by when? What will you need, and by when?

Two of the major areas that need planning are people and resources. In terms of people, this includes youth workers, young people, parents and guardians, guest speakers, and other specialists. It requires an awareness of the church calendar when scheduling events. In terms of resources, you need to plan such things as the curriculum, venue hire, transportation, finance and fundraising, and publicity and promotion.

You may find it helpful to work backwards from your intended outcome, identifying all the different and sequential stages or processes that will be required. By putting a date to each stage, you will see how long the whole process will realistically take. This is called Critical Path Analysis (CPA).

Maintaining flexibility

Plans you follow rigidly are almost as unhelpful as non-existent plans. Things won't always go to plan. Introducing minor – or occasionally significant – changes can steer the group back on course. Having SMART goals makes it easier to monitor progress. Youth work and ministry, with its values of voluntary participation, informal education and empowerment, thrives on spontaneity. Your planning process must allow for this.

A sudden fall of snow could be a great opportunity to gather everyone available to go tobogganing. Similarly, what better way to cool off on an unexpectedly hot summer's day than with a water fight? British weather is too unreliable to plan such events with any certainty. New or improved plans must still take into full account 'good practice' principles. You are no less responsible for replacement activities than for ongoing, routine ones.

To think about...
How comfortable do you feel with detailed planning responsibilities? When is the most productive time to do your planning? How flexible are you in your youth work and ministry?

Keeping the rhythm

Groups thrive on rhythm. It enables them to develop a sustainable life of their own. But watch out for the 'Curse of the Successful Experience'. You experience a frisson of satisfaction after a great session, but rapidly succumb to the pressure to go one better next time. Then you find yourself with an unhealthy expectation, which is a recipe for boredom. There are only so many times you can visit the country's best theme park before it becomes just another routine. Instead, you should plan to intersperse routine activities with surprises. These will keep the group interested and create shared memories.

You should avoid scheduling themes that last a whole term, as these can become monotonous. Twelve weeks

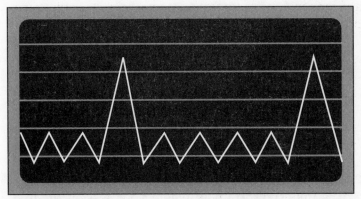

A healthy programme with occasional surprises.

looking at Ecclesiastes is likely to be more than the young people can bear.

Some young people have full diaries. Knowing that youth group is every Thursday from 7.30pm till 9.30pm helps both them and their parents plan their time. Other young people have too much spare time, and the regularity of Thursday evenings gives them something to look forward to. It rarely helps to keep changing the day or time the group meets. Even varying the venue can cause difficulties. It is far better to settle on the day and time suitable for most, and stick to it.

There are seasons to youth work and ministry. Generally, attendance at centre-based activities rises in the winter and falls in the summer. Include this in your planning, increasing the number of indoor activities and staff during the winter and switching to more outdoor work in the summer. Remember, incarnational youth work and ministry goes to where the young people are.

Preparing a session

Here are some tips for your planning and delivery of the sessions in your programme schedule.

1. *Accepting the challenge*

It is both a privilege and an awesome responsibility to work with young people. They deserve the best you can offer. You should take the role as seriously as if you were leading Sunday morning worship at your church. The quality of your preparation will determine the effectiveness of your delivery.

2. *Recognising the context*

It is important to know where your session fits into the term's programme, and what contribution it makes towards your aim(s) and goals. How will you link this to what precedes and follows it? You should also plan each session to meet the needs of the age group you serve.

Younger groups generally need more:	Older groups generally need more:
Structured time.	Unstructured time.
Active and faster-paced sessions, with lots of varied things to do.	Involvement in decision-making.
Emphasis on doing and less reliance on discussing.	Discussion opportunities.
Variety in a series and shorter sessions.	Opportunities to ask questions and solve problems.
Competitive team activities.	On-going projects that require their time and skill.
Events they can invite their friends to.	Interaction with youth workers.
On-site activities.	Off-site activities.
Same-sex activities.	Mixed-sex activities.

3. *Obtaining the resources*

There is no point devising an imaginative and challenging session that requires materials or props you don't have and can't get. What resources will you need to complete the planned activities? Where and when will you obtain them? The further ahead you plan, the greater the chance of obtaining what you require. If you don't have it, someone, somewhere will. Email your contacts. Keep a handy supply of paper, pens, Youth Bibles and other commonly required resources in a stacker box. Ask your church to provide a youth budget, enabling you to purchase resources as required.

4. *Keeping it safe*

You will need to consider the 'safe practice' requirements for each session. If an activity requires more people than you have co-workers, for example, can you enlist a few volunteers for that session? Remember to plan how you will effectively supervise them. How will you manage the building and equipment to ensure the safety of the young people, youth workers and other building users? If the session involves a trip, how and when will you secure parental/guardian consent and what form of transportation will you use? Is the planned activity covered by your organisation's Public Liability and Personal Accident insurance policy?

5. *Constructing the outline*

As with a novel, beginnings and endings are important. What will you do when the session starts to grab the attention and interest of your young people? Similarly, what will you do at the end to send them out with positive memories of what they have done and learnt? You should plan how you will promote young people's participation. Even Saint Paul couldn't stop young Eutychus from falling asleep during a long-winded monologue (Acts 20:9). Where possible, use interactive and informal methods to educate, such as role-play, group work, problem-solving, discussions and so forth. But be careful not to allow a creative idea to hide the session's contents. The aim is not to show how funny you can be but to create a lively environment for young people's development.

6. *Involving others*

Don't assume that you are the only one capable of delivering part or all of the session. Do you know an individual or organisation that could provide some specialist knowledge or experience? Guests provide young people with variety, give youth workers a break and help to forge links beyond the group. Make sure you adequately brief your guest about what she or he is expected to do and with whom.

7. *Getting going*

It is important that you and your co-workers arrive in good time – before the session starts. You need to be totally focused on the young people when they turn up. Give yourselves 30 minutes to prepare. This is normally enough time for last minute chores, organisation of the venue and a quick team meeting (including prayer) to confirm who has responsibility for what during the session.

During the session you will need to be flexible with all that you have prepared. Remember, the values of youth work and ministry call for you to make the most of opportunities that arise. Inevitably, your multi-tasking will include looking out for visitors and those outside of a peer group, monitoring the safety of the group and facilities, having conversations with individuals and facilitating the session's content.

At the end of the session, it is important to conduct a short debrief with your co-workers. This will help you and the group to grow from each session. Ask questions such as – What lessons can be learnt from the organisation for next time? What worked well and what didn't? What issues need to be dealt with and by whom? What is happening next session and who is taking responsibility for what?

To think about...
Think back to a session that you consider to have been particularly good. What happened? What made the session so positive? What did you learn from this?

Ideas and resources

Thinking creatively

With practice and the right approach, everyone can think creatively. After all, we are made in the image of the Creator God. Here are two methods to get you started.

1. Brainstorming

This technique enables groups of people to generate ideas and information as quickly as possible – evaluation is left till afterwards. Use brainstorming to generate ideas for a term's programme, a session plan or an individual activity. Set a time and space limit, and designate one person to record the output onto a large sheet or board. This person must record everything that is said without prejudice. Deciding what is useful is strictly for later.

In a good brainstorm, ideas are thrown in without analysis. There is no right or wrong at this stage; no ideas are justified, or challenged, by anyone; it is briskly and light-heartedly facilitated, and it should be fun to do; it is quick, lasting no more than 20 minutes; and all ideas and observations are recorded for all to see. Once completed, participants review the content of their brainstorm to see what ideas and observations are most relevant.

2. *Mind mapping*

With frequent use, it is possible to train your mind to think creatively. If brainstorming is for groups, then mind mapping[1] is for individuals. This technique releases your brain to explore themes, plus related words and images. It begins with a central image or theme, for example 'happiness'. From this the key headings or Basic Ordering Ideas are formed, such as 'people' and 'activities'. These give rise to new spin-off ideas that can in turn prompt further spin-offs. This can continue indefinitely, but is stopped when helpful ideas and content are unearthed.

Though the process can be done on paper, you can train your brain to do it automatically using a combination of

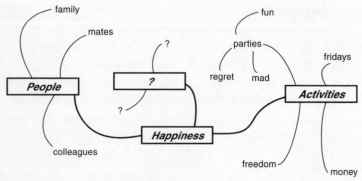

associated words and images. It's a bit like letting your mind go for a walk and seeing where it ends up.

In addition to your own ideas and those provided in the Ideas Factory, use the resources of Youthwork – the Partnership.

Ideas

Coming up with creative and practical ideas each week can be draining. Youth workers are often only as good as the last idea they copied, bought or stole. Here are a few places to start looking.

1. *Magazines*

Youthwork Magazine is published monthly and is Britain's most widely read magazine resource for equipping and informing Christian youth workers. It provides ideas, resources and guidance for youth ministry. Each edition includes a number of ready-to-use session outlines.

2. *Conferences*

Youthwork – the Conference is an annual weekend conference that inspires, equips, resources and networks all those involved with youth work and ministry. Your church denomination or network may also provide regional events.

3. *Books*

Youthwork – the Resources is a series of books written for those involved in youth work and ministry. 'Resourcing Ministry' titles, such as Steve Adam's *Music That Moves the Soul*,[2] provide busy youth workers with tried and tested ideas and curriculum.

Youth Specialties also produce a range of books aimed at the American market.

4. *Websites*
   Youthwork – the Website at www.youthwork.co.uk
   has information, resources, community, learning and
   opportunities.

Conclusion

This concludes not only Chapter Nine but also the book's
narrative. All that remains is for you to put what you have
read into practice. You and your youth work and ministry
will never be the same again.

In the final part, 'Resourcing', you will find many
tried and tested ideas for you to use with your group,
together with a Resource Directory listing a number of
useful organisations and resources.

Summary

● Developing a programme starts with knowing your
  aim(s) and SMART goals:
  ○ Simple
  ○ Measurable
  ○ Achievable
  ○ Realistic
  ○ Time-specific
● Involving young people in the decision-making proc-
  ess promotes their own development and ensures the
  programmes remains relevant to their needs.
● A balanced programme meets young people's physical,
  social, emotional, moral and spiritual developmental
  needs.
● Planning ahead reduces stress.

- Informal education requires there to be a high degree of flexibility.
- Keeping a group's rhythm increases participation and reduces boredom.
- To plan an effective session, you need to accept the challenge, know your context, obtain the resources in plenty of time, plan 'good practice', construct the outline, involve others and get going in good time.
- You can increase your creativity through brainstorming in groups and mind mapping on your own.
- Most ideas are borrowed, bought or stolen. Knowing where to look can make all the difference.

NOTES

1. For a detailed introduction to mind mapping read *The Mind Map Book* by Tony & Barry Buzan (BBC Worldwide, 2000).
2. Adams, S., *Music that Moves the Soul* (Authentic, 2003).

Part Four

RESOURCING

10

Ideas factory

10 ideas for warm-up icebreakers

1. Pairs² (Pairs Squared)
- Ask participants to organise themselves into pairs and introduce themselves to their partner.
- Ask each pair to join up with another pair and instruct them to swap partners so that each person is now paired up with someone different.
- Ask the partners to link arms. You are now ready to play tag.
- Without breaking the link, each person must attempt to tag their original partner (and no one else).
- If someone is tagged, both members of the pair must stop and turn 360 degrees before resuming the game.
- Set a time and space limit, and ensure no running.

2. Heads or tails?
- Demonstrate two positions: 'heads', a hand on the top of your head; and 'tails', a hand on your gluteus (buttock).
- When you shout 'heads' or 'tails' everyone must immediately adopt the relevant position. For added pace, ask participants to decide as you throw a coin in the air.
- Those with a hand on their head then declare themselves to be the heads teams. Those with a hand on their gluteus declare themselves to be the tails team.

- Play a game of tag, deciding whether heads or tails are 'it'.
- Once a head tags a tail, the tail becomes a head (and vice versa).
- Continue the game until all tails or heads have been tagged.
- Repeat the game, randomly varying your selection of the 'it' team.

3. Number Cruncher
- Ask participants to sit in a circle.
- Ask them to 'number off', counting in a clockwise direction.
- Any number that contains a seven or is a multiple of seven must be replaced with a word or phrase (you choose what) and the direction reversed.
- 1, 2, 3, 4, 5, 6, [word], 8, 9, 10, 11, 12, 13, [word], 15, 16, [word], 18...

4. Alienation
- Select someone as an 'alien' but don't let the others know who.
- Secretly supply the 'alien' with lots of easily identifiable tags (e.g. brightly coloured paperclips or washers).
- The alien's mission is to secretly neutralise the other participants by tagging them without being seen by anyone. Ideally participants should find the tag long after it has been delivered.
- If challenged, the alien will need to bluff.
- At close of the meeting, find out who has been neutralised and reveal the identity of the alien.

5. Life lines
- Invite young people to chart their lives, pinpointing the significant events on maps you provide. To promote diversity, give each person photocopies of a world and national map.
- Using a marker-pen, each young person should mark and date their birthplace. Then they should draw a line (with a date) to another location that is significant to them. This

process should be repeated until their lifeline reaches the ongoing small or cell group meeting. Significant places could include towns where they have lived, memorable holidays, family influences, and so on.

- Invite each person to talk the group through their lifeline. Use the opportunity to foster conversation.

6. *Limbs*

- If your group is large, ask the young people to organise themselves into teams of six. Their challenge is to stand together with as few of their limbs touching the floor as possible. They can stand on each other's feet. Give them five minutes to plan their strategy. Take care to ensure groups remain safe.

7. *Identity parade*

- Ask the young people to organise themselves in two facing lines. Select one line as 'observers' and the other as 'changers'. Give the 'observers' 60 seconds to study the 'changers' before turning their backs on them.
- The 'changers' now have 60 seconds to change ten things about their appearance or organisation. The changes must be visible and could be applied to just one participant or spread out across the whole line.
- The 'observers' turn back to face the 'changers'. They have 60 seconds to identify the ten changes.
- Afterwards swap roles, with the 'observers' becoming the 'changers' and vice versa.

8. *Musical papers*

- Place some sheets of paper on the floor. Play some music and invite the young people to circulate. When the music stops the young people must ensure their feet are on paper and not touching the floor. After each round, remove one sheet of paper and fold the others in half. Continue until no one is able to stand on the paper without touching the floor.

9. *Balloon basketball/netball*

- Divide the group into two equally sized teams and the room into two halves. Ask each team to select a 'hoop'; this person should stand on a chair/low table in their opponent's half and form the shape of a basketball/netball hoop. On your whistle, the teams must work together to score by getting the balloon into their hoop. Stress that this is a non-contact sport; no one should wrestle the balloon from the hands of another player.

10. *Paper towers*

- Provide the group(s) with a large quantity of newspapers and tape. Give them a time and space limit in which to construct the tallest, freestanding tower using only the materials provided.

10 ideas to promote initiative

1. *Hammer balance*

- Provide the group/teams with a wooden or steel 30cm ruler, a claw hammer and a 40-50cm length of string/shoe lace.
- Using only the materials provided, suspend all the objects in mid-air. Only the first 3cm of the ruler may touch the edge of a table; nothing else may touch the ruler, hammer or string.
- The key is physics. Tie the string into a loop and drape it over the ruler at approximately the 15cm mark. Now loop

the other end around the hammer and, holding the ruler in place, allow the hammer to tilt downwards so that its handle is wedged against the tip of the ruler. Adjust the string until you achieve perfect equilibrium.

2. *Group lines*

• Challenge the group/teams to organise themselves into lines of descending order in complete silence. Categories could include height, age, length of time associated with the group/church.

3. *Bucket lift*

• Create a large circle on the ground using either rope or chalk and designate this 'the danger zone'. Put a valuable object in a bucket in the middle of the danger zone. Provide the group/teams with an assortment of props, including an elastic tie (the kind used to fix items to roof racks) and various long lengths of standard rope.

• Challenge the group/teams to retrieve the valuable object without anything or anyone at any time touching the ground in the danger zone. Anything or anyone that does should be permanently removed from the task.

• For added complexity, set a time limit and/or instruct the group/teams to act in complete silence.

• The clue is in looping the rope through the elastic tie and stretching it. Maintain the tension and manoeuvre the extended tie over the bucket. Once in position, gradually relax the tension (being careful not to let any rope touch the ground within the danger zone) until the tie tightens around the bucket. Then lift the bucket off the ground and out of the danger zone. Obviously this won't work if the elastic is too long to tighten around the bucket, so check the length first and shorten it if necessary.

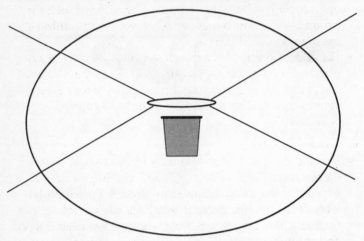

4. *Balloon platoon*

- Ask the group/teams to stand in a single file and give each person a balloon to blow up and tie.
- Use the balloons to join everyone together like XoXoXoX. No one may touch a balloon with their hand and no balloon should be dropped or burst. The participants must work together, using their bodies to wedge the balloons in place.
- Challenge the group/teams to journey across the room or even around the building. If anyone drops or touches their balloon with their hands, the whole platoon must go back to the beginning and start again.
- For added complexity, introduce corners, stairs or even a simple obstacle.

5. *Stepping Stones*

- Mark out on the ground a large 'danger zone'.
- Provide a 'stepping stone' for all but one of the group/

teams. Suitable 'stones' include carpet tiles and blocks of wood.

- Challenge the group/teams to get across the danger zone using only their stepping stones. The whole team must cross together. Only the stepping stones may touch the ground within the danger zone. Anyone or anything else must go back and start again.
- For added complexity, for each stepping stone to remain effective it must have constant direct contact with one of the participants. Any stepping stone that loses contact should be returned to the beginning or permanently removed.

6. *Mountain rescue*
- Provide the group/teams with an assortment of equipment and resources that any self-respecting mountain expedition might be expected to possess. For example, tent, sleeping bags, plastic bivvy bags, rucksacks etc...
- Set the scene. One member of the group has been injured and is unable to walk. The weather is deteriorating and they urgently need medical attention. The rest of the group must devise a means to transport them down the mountain to safety using only the equipment and resources they have with them.
- To avoid damage to expensive equipment, use replacement materials. For example, using an old sheet for a tent.
- Ask the group at different stages to explain their actions and the rationale for them.
- The purpose of this exercise is for the group to work together; not to recreate the level of risk an actual mountain rescue would entail. Be sure to closely monitor the risk to the group, and especially to the 'casualty' being transported. If in doubt, don't.

7. *Mine Field*
- Mark out an area using chalk, rope or tape, and declare this to be a minefield.
- Blindfold all but one of the participants and position them in the minefield, all in different positions and facing

in various directions. Scatter a number of mines (e.g. tennis balls) throughout the area.

- The sighted participant must stand outside of the minefield and guide those inside to safety by shouting instructions to them. Those in the minefield must only move on instruction from the guide, who must only move one participant one step at a time.
- Anyone who touches a mine should be removed from the activity.
- For added complexity, select two people to be the guide: one can speak but cannot see, having their back to the minefield; the other can see but cannot speak. How will they communicate with each other, and those in the minefield?

8. *Spider's web*

- Use a long rope or chord strung between two trees to create a spider's web.
- Declare the spider's web to be highly toxic. It blocks the path of the participants. They can't go over it, and they can't go under it. They have to go through it.
- Participants must work together to navigate through the spider's web, taking extreme care not to touch the toxic web.

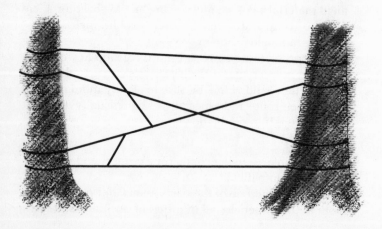

9. *Holy water*
- Obtain a tall piece of plastic piping and drill a large number of holes of varying sizes in it. Cap one end of the pipe.
- Pour a full bucket of water into the pipe. Participants must stop the water from leaking out. After three minutes, empty what's left of the water back into the bucket and see how much they have retained.

10. *The Great Egg Race*
- Give people a small ball and an assortment of objects and materials such as string, plastic sheeting, bamboo canes, coat hanger etc.
- Using only the materials provided, challenge the participants to construct a run that transports the ball the greatest possible distance. The ball should be able to travel without external help.

10 ideas to promote outreach

1. *What would Jesus say to… ?*
Some young people struggle to see the relevance of Christian faith to modern life. Invite them to organise a debate about what Jesus would say to famous media personalities and politicians. To be effective, the young people will need to carefully research both the personalities under review and the teachings of Christ. What is this person really like? What sort of conversation would they have with Jesus? It is important to remember that Jesus, as with the Samaritan woman (John 4), would probably have both affirming and challenging things to say – but always in a positive way.

2. *Tell me a story*
Stories are not just for children; everyone can benefit from them. What's more, everyone has got a story to tell. Encourage young people to tell their stories on video by

creating a Big Brother-style diary room. You may want
to suggest a number of categories, such as embarrassing,
heavy, funny, significant, sad, happy, etc. Listening to their
stories will create an opportunity for you to tell your story
– all of which connects to God's story.

3. Three-story evangelism
YfC have developed a three-story approach to evangelism.
This enables young people to listen to their friend's story
and connect this to their own story – all with the aim of
connecting God's story to their friend's story. YfC have produced a package and an accompanying book that you can
use with your young people.

4. Go fishing
Fishing is for people who have patience and worms by the
bucket-load. Activities like this can create a great opportunity to involve a few young people in your hobby and create
space to discuss life, the universe and skateboarding. Don't
forget to consider the 'safe practice' implications.

5. Community Service
Young people of all backgrounds and spiritual interests can
benefit from participating in community service projects
such as the Faithworks in the Community weeks organised
by Oasis on behalf of the Faithworks Movement. In the
1990s more young people came to faith through the Oasis
Christmas Cracker 'eat less, pay more' projects than through
the high tech Video Express and Video Wall evangelism
teams. Why? Because Christian and non-Christian young
people and youth workers gained mutual respect and
understanding as they cooked, cleaned, washed and peeled.

6. Host an Alpha for Youth course
The Alpha Course, developed by Holy Trinity, Brompton,
has had a significant impact across the world and been
adopted by a diverse range of Christian denominations and
networks. A youth-friendly version of the course is now
available for 11-14s and 15-18s, complete with leaders' manu-
als. Order it online from www.wesleyowen.com

7. *Take 'em away*

Residential experiences can often be very significant in the life of individuals and groups. They create space and freedom to chat, reflect and bond. For example, YfC organise action-packed Fort Rocky weekends, designed specifically to further young people's spiritual journey. What's more, accompanying workers can simply turn up and enjoy time spent with their young people, leaving the programme delivery to YfC.

8. *Go surfing*

When considering spiritual matters, some young people prefer the anonymity that the internet offers. There are a number of Christian websites that young people may find helpful. Check these out for yourself before recommending them:

- www.life2themax.co.uk (younger focus)
- www.rejesus.co.uk
- www.church.co.uk (older focus)

9. *Commercial Christmas*

Every Christmas the Churches' Advertising Network sponsors a national billboard poster and radio advertising campaign to make people think about Christ. The current and previous campaigns are available at www.churchads.org.uk. Encourage your core members to download and distribute these amongst their friends, creating a viral media effect. In addition, use the posters and radio adverts as discussion starters with individuals and groups of young people.

10. *Play football*

There are local football leagues just about everywhere. As you connect with a group of hard-to-reach young people, consider enabling them to form a football team and enter the local league. Contact Sport England, the Football Association, Christians in Sport and your Local Authority Leisure Department for information and resources. Of course, it needn't be football, nor should it be just for boys/young men.

10 ideas to promote small groups

1. Play Jenga

Obtain a Jenga set – the game of building blocks – and use it to form the basis of your cell group session.

Welcome: As each member arrives, give them a handful of Jenga blocks. When the group is complete play a game of Jenga.

Worship: Read a Bible passage that focuses on the cross of Christ. Invite the group to reflect and pray, using their Jenga blocks to form a large wooden cross on the floor.

Word: Select a few key words from the Bible reading. Challenge the group to spell out each word using all their Jenga blocks. Try making this into a time-trial. As each word is formed, ask questions that enable the group to say what its relevance is.

Witness: Invite each member to write on the Jenga blocks the names – or initials – of those people they know who could become group members. Take a few minutes to pray for each name.

2. Make a video

- Select a Bible passage for the group to reflect upon e.g. Psalm 139. Ask them to bring to the next group session some video or TV footage that could be incorporated into a short video montage to accompany the reading.
- At a basic level, it is possible to edit material by connecting two video recorders together. Played back with the TV sound off, the video montage can accompany the reading and/or music from CD or tape player. However, more sophisticated editing is now readily available using a home computer.
- Thinking about which images to use will enable the group to reflect on, and debate, the Bible passage.

3. Buy a cow or some chickens

- Challenge your young people to purchase a cow or some chickens for a community in a developing country. You

can do this through a world development organisation
such as World Vision. Use this as an opportunity to discover more about life in another context and promote the
spiritual discipline of giving.

4. *Small group Olympics*
- Host an alternative Olympics in which each event
  requires minimum activity. These might include little-
  finger wrestling, ten-metre walkathon, throwing the
  matchstick, synchronised sitting, and so on. This surreal
  event works best if everyone is in sports kit. Provide
  small awards for the least amount of effort invested.
- An alternative is to ask each person to bring a sleeping-
  bag and host a Sleeping Bag Olympics, with each event
  contested in the sleeping bags. Examples are high-jump-
  ing, sprinting, gymnastics and volleyball.

5. *Watch a film*
- Take the group to the cinema to see an age-appropriate
  film. Alternatively, rent a video. Afterwards, take time to
  review the film.
- Use this as an opportunity for conversation and encourage your young people to be aware of the influences
  – good and bad – that the media often have. What key
  issues did the film highlight? What aspects of God's character were mirrored by parts of the film? What aspects of
  the film were challenges to God's nature? What overall
  rating do you give the film?

6. *Play Scrabble*
Obtain a game of Scrabble® and use it to form the basis of
the cell group session.
- Welcome: As each member arrives, ask them to register
  by spelling out their name on the board using the
  Scrabble letters. Depending on how much time you have
  available, begin a game of Scrabble.
- Worship: Invite members to spell out prayers using the
  Scrabble pieces. Read an appropriate Bible passage.
- Word: Once you have taken a few minutes to outline the
  basis of the teaching, invite the group to play a game of

Scrabble, with double-scores given for words relevant to the session theme. Use the opportunity to ask probing questions that build young people's understanding and awareness.

- Witness: Invite members of the group to spell out the names – or initials – of people they are currently praying for. Conclude by praying for each person named.

7. *Watch a match*

- Arrange to watch a local match – this might be amateur/ semiprofessional football/netball or a school match. If a group member is playing, it is always encouraging if the rest of the group turns up to watch and cheer them on from the sidelines.

8. *Serve the community*

- Empower the group to develop a community project. They will need to begin by researching the needs in your neighbourhood, before deciding what they can deliver. Use this as an opportunity to develop organisational skills, spiritual maturity and community awareness. Be sure to emphasise the importance of servanthood and sustainability.
- Specially prepared resources are available from www.oasistrust.org/passion/
- Alternatively, consider participating as a group in a local volunteering scheme. Contact your local Council for Voluntary Service www.nacvs.org.uk/cvsdir/ to see what options are available.

9. *Lead worship*

- Work together to plan a worship service. Make sure to secure a suitable date some months in advance and use the time to plan well.

10. *Go rock climbing*

- There are many indoor rock-climbing walls that you can hire. Use this activity to create a memorable experience, group bonding and maybe an opportunity to talk about fears, trust and stepping out.

- Make sure to enlist an appropriately qualified, equipped and insured instructor. Most Local Education Authorities have an outdoor education coordinator, who will be able to advise you on locations and instructors. Alternatively, contact the Adventure Activities Licensing Authority (see the Resources Directory).

10 ideas to promote prayer

1. Jenga Prayers
Obtain a Jenga set – the game of building blocks – and use it to form the basis of your cell group session.

Welcome: As each member arrives, give them a handful of Jenga blocks. When the group is complete play a game of Jenga.

Worship: Read a Bible passage that focuses on the cross of Christ. Invite the group to reflect and pray, using their Jenga blocks to form a large wooden cross on the floor.

Word: Select a few key words from the Bible reading. Challenge the group to spell out each word using all their Jenga blocks. Try making this into a time-trial. As each word is formed, ask questions that enable the group to say what its relevance is.

Witness: Invite each member to write on the Jenga blocks the names – or initials – of those people they know who could become group members. Take a few minutes to pray for each name.

2. 24-7 Prayer
- 24-7 began in 1999 with a single prayer room set up by the young people of Revelation Church, Chichester. In this room they prayed without ceasing in one-hour shifts for several weeks, inspired by the example of the 18th-century Moravians. As people were attracted to the prayer room, word spread and the idea caught on in other churches as well as on university campuses. There has been a 24-7 Prayer Room in 45 nations, in

most denominations and in venues as diverse as the U.S. Naval Academy and a German Punk Festival. For further information about setting up a 24-7 Prayer Room visit www.24-7prayer.com

3. *Woolly prayers*
- Obtain a large ball of wool and arrange the group in a circle. Tie one end of the wool around your ankle or wrist and lead the group in a short prayer. Call someone by name and throw the ball of wool to them. This person must wrap the wool around a part of their body and lead the group in another short prayer. They then repeat the process by throwing the ball of wool to another group member. Continue until you have run out of wool and the group is completely entwined.

4. *Global prayers*
- Borrow a large inflatable earth ball and use this as a focus for world prayer. Ask the young people to research topics for prayer by watching the news or reading the newspapers. Lay hands on the earth ball as you pray for the different countries. The Central Intelligence Service website www.cia.gov is a good source of information. Visit www.gmi.org/ow/ or obtain a copy of Operation World by Patrick Johnstone and Jason Mandryk (Authentic/ WEC, 2001) for detailed information on, and the prayer needs of, every country in the world.

5. *Takeaway prayers*
- Most town and city high streets have a number of fast food or take-away outlets. Visit each one with your young people, sample their food and pray outside for the relevant country. For example, pray for Italy outside the pizza place, for China outside the Chinese take-away and just about anywhere you choose outside McDonalds.

6. *Prayer letters*
- Find a large open space and invite your young people, working together as a team, to create prayer letters by spelling out key words using their bodies. For example,

call out 'peace' and have the young people position themselves to spell out the word – and then suggest they pray
for peace.

7. *Dark Prayers*
* Find some fluorescent paint and reflective strips. Grab
  a stack of large sheets of black paper or card. Invite the
  group to create key words on the card using the paint
  and strips. The words could relate to a Bible passage
  you have been studying. Once completed, display the
  cards on the walls. Close the curtains and shut the doors,
  blocking out as much sunlight as possible – the darker the
  better. With the lights off, invite someone to read the Bible
  passage using a low-powered torch to see. The key words
  should be highly visible in the darkened room. Take time
  to reflect and to pray.

8. *Street prayers*
* Psalms were expressive prayers written by real people
  facing times of both joy and pain. Invite the young people
  to write psalm prayers using whichever language style
  they feel most comfortable with. For example, they could
  use rap, drum 'n' bass or even street art (graffiti).

9. *Lord's Prayer*
* Use the Lord's Prayer to create a structure for prayer.
  Within each section create space for food, prayer, games
  and Bible readings.
      Our Father in heaven…
          Prayers of worship and praise
      your kingdom come…
          Prayers for justice
      Give us this day our daily bread.
          Prayers for famine victims in Africa
      Forgive us our debts,
          Prayers for the release of third world debt in Asia
      as we also have forgiven our debtors.
          Child prostitution or homelessness in South America
      And lead us not into temptation…
          Prayers for materialistic Europe

> For yours is the kingdom…
> > *Prayers of thanks.*

10. *Famous prayers*
- Write down the name of a famous living personality from the world of media, sports or politics on a post-it note and stick it on the back of a young person without them being able to read the name. Do the same for all the young people, using a different living personality for each. The young people have to guess the identity of the person written on their back by listening to what others pray. This activity works best if all the young people mingle and pray for each other's famous personality.

10 ideas to promote use of the Bible

1. *Bible drums*
- Drummers have often felt sidelined or been the butt of jokes. (What's the difference between a drummer and a drum machine? With a drum machine, you only have to punch the beat in once.)
- Psalm Drummers is a worldwide network of drummers and percussionists (posh drummers) who use drumming to create unity and influence change. For thousands of years people have used drums to announce the coming of man. Psalm Drummers use the drum to announce God's coming. They use their skills and instruments to interpret Psalms from the Bible. To find out how your drummers could get involved, visit www.psalmdrummers.com

2. *Bible text*
- Text messaging with mobile phones is changing the way we communicate as well as the way we write. The original limitation of just 160 characters or digits per message led to the development of 'text speak'.
- A national competition challenged people to 'text' the Lord's Prayer using just 160 digits. The winner began "HI PA U R IN HVN".

- Challenge your group to translate a passage of the Bible into text speak. End by sending the text to each other or to people outside of the group.

3. *Bible-a-thon*

- The Bible can appear dauntingly long for many young people, but the New Testament can be read in just nine hours and the whole Bible in 27 hours. Challenge your young people to prove it can be done. Organise a 'lock-in' or residential weekend and as part of this designate a room for Bible reading. Fill it with paper, pens, paints and Bibles. Invite young people to fill 30-minute slots around the clock to ensure that someone is continually reading the Bible throughout the event.

4. *Bible Society*

- The Bible Society promotes awareness and use of the Bible. Their website includes interactive games, presentations and facts. Visit www.biblesociety.org.uk

5. *Walk thru the Bible*

- Most young people (and adults) struggle to understand how the various books of the Bible hang together. They know that it begins with Genesis and ends with Revelation, with Jesus coming somewhere in the middle, but the rest is a bit hazy. Provide your young people with a Bible overview that takes them on a whistle-stop tour of the whole book. Walk Thru the Bible Ministries provide memorable workshops and resources. Visit them at www.bible.org.uk or call 01255 850600.

6. *Word-on-the-web*

- Remembering to read the Bible every day can be a discipline that some young people (and adults) find difficult to establish. Encourage your young people to subscribe to receive a daily short reading and lively comment from www.word-on-the-web.co.uk – free, simple and easy to read.

7. *Daily Word*

- Provide newspapers and ask the young people to identify

some of the more interesting and important reports. Set
the challenge of discovering what the Bible has to say
about these situations. Provide a supply of Bible aids,
such as concordances and Bible dictionaries. Of particular
help are *The Complete Book of Everyday Christianity* by
Robert Banks and Paul Stevens (IVP, 1997) and *The New
Dictionary of Christian Ethics and Pastoral Theology* by David
Atkinson and David Field (IVP, 1995). Conclude the session by asking the young people to present the news and
incorporate a biblical response.

8. *Bible sponsors*
- There are a number of youth Bibles on the market specifically designed to help young people get into the word.
  Aim to stock a number of copies for the group. Better
  still, give every group member a free copy. Your local
  Christian bookshop may be willing to provide a discount
  for bulk orders. To do this, invite members of the congregation to sponsor copies.

9. *Location, location, location*
- If the youth budget (another bad joke) does not stretch
  to taking the group to the Holy Land, then use locations
  nearer to home. For example, take the group on either a
  picnic or to a McDonalds and talk about the feeding of
  the 5,000. Be creative with your location Bible studies.

10. *Word on the street*
- Lend the young people a camcorder and show them how
  to use it properly. Ask them to find out what members of
  the public think about a topic you will be looking at in
  the group. For example, 'What gives you hope?' or 'What
  are good friends like?'

10 ideas to boost your own spirituality

1. *Word-on-the-web*
- Subscribe to receive daily devotional Bible studies sent

from www.word-on-the-web.co.uk to your email inbox at home or work. They're free, short and simple to use.

2. *Get a dog*
- Responsible dog owners make time to walk their four-legged friends at least once a day. As well as keeping fit, it also creates sacred space for prayer and reflection. If you don't want the responsibility of owning a dog, borrow one from a neighbour.

3. *Read a book*
- Visit your local Christian bookshop or www.wesleyowen.com.
- Find a time and place that fits with your lifestyle. For example, whilst commuting (not driving), during a lunch break (go on, take one), or on holiday.

4. *Youthwork – the Conference*
- Plan to attend Youthwork – the Conference, the annual weekend conference designed to inspire, equip, resource and network volunteer youth workers. Select options that will feed your soul, not just those that will improve your practice. See www.youthworkconference.co.uk

5. *Buy some ice lollies*
- Write the names of those you wish to pray for on lolly sticks. Place them in a jar next to the kettle or bathroom mirror and make it your habit each time you pass by to pull out a couple of sticks and pray for those named.

6. *Form a cell group*
- Form a small group or cell with your fellow volunteer youth workers. Not only will this enhance your team work, foster friendship and save you time, it will also promote your accountability and spirituality.

7. *Throw a dinner party*
- Jesus shared many meals with friends and strangers. Make it your habit to invite people round for meals. Enjoy the conversation and the opportunity to entertain angels (Heb 13:2) or even Jesus (Mt. 25:34–40).

8. *Read the Bible as a novel*

- Sometimes, by reading only occasional or isolated chapters and verses it can be difficult to follow the unfolding story of the Bible. Counter this by reading the Bible as a novel. CWR produce a chronological reading plan called *Cover to Cover* by Selwyn Hughes and Trevor Partridge (CWR, 1999).

9. *Experience a different expression of faith*

- Create an opportunity to experience a different Christian tradition's worship service. If you are from a charismatic or Pentecostal tradition, considering visiting an Orthodox community. If you are from a high church tradition, consider visiting a new or house church. Alternatively, seek a different ethnic or international tradition. For example, visit a black majority church or a French-speaking congregation. Expect to encounter God even in services where the language spoken is not your own. Allow the new experience to encourage and challenge your own approach to faith and spirituality.

10. *Go online*

- www.church.co.uk is a one-stop shop for exploring Christian faith. It's for everyone who wants to talk about life, faith and Christianity. It's a safe place to explore beliefs, doubts and questions about Christian spirituality.
- www.rejesus.co.uk provides a creative and diverse range of resources
- Labyrinth is an online version of the Cathedral Labyrinth created by London alternative worship groups Grace, LOPE, and Epicentre and touring UK Cathedrals with YfC. The original is described as 'an interactive installation for spiritual journeys'. It consists of a pathway mapped out on the floor for visitors to follow. During this journey participants pause and listen to a piece of music and a meditation. They also undertake some symbolic action or ritual.

11

Resource directory

This list is by no means exhaustive. Please note, whilst every effort has been made to ensure the accuracy of information, details inevitably change with time. The author and publishers accept no liability for any loss or damage of any kind that may arise from any error or omission.

Church Youth Networks

1. **Assemblies of God**
   Contact: Simon Jarvis (National Director)
   Visit: www.youth-alive.co.uk
   Email: info@youth-alive.co.uk
   Call: (+44) 02476740794
   Write to: Youth Alive, Old School House, 15 Bulkington Road, Bedworth, Warwickshire, CV12 9DG.

2. **Baptist Union of Great Britain**
   Contact: Nick Lear (Mission Advisor)
   Visit: www.baptist.org.uk
   Email: nlear@baptist.org.uk
   Call: (+44) 01235 517700
   Write to: Nick Lear, Baptist House, PO Box 44, 129 Broadway, Didcot, Oxfordshire, OX11 8RT.

3. **Baptist Union of Scotland**
   Contact: Gary Smith (Youth Advisor)
   Visit: www.busy.org.uk
   Email: gary@busy.org.uk
   Call: (+44) 0141 423 6169
   Write to: Youth Office, Baptist Union of Scotland, 14 Aytoun Road, Glasgow, G41 5RT.

4. Church in Wales
Contact: Pam Richards (Interim Provincial Youth Officer)
Visit: www.churchinwales.org.uk/cmm
Email: Youth.cmm@churchinwales.org.uk
Call: (+44) 02920 348200
Write to: 39 Cathedral Road, Cardiff, CF11 9XF.

5. Church of England
Contact: Peter Ball/ Yvonne Criddle (National Youth Officers)
Visit: www.cofe.anglican.org/about/education
Email: peter.ball@c-of-e.org.uk / yvonne.criddle@c-of-
           e.org.uk
Call: (+44) 0207 898 1000
Write to: Church of England Youth Service, Church House,
           Great Smith Street, London SW1P 3NZ.

6. Church of Ireland
Contact: David Brown (Youth Ministry Co-ordinator)
Visit: www.ciyd.org
Email: ciydn@ireland.anglican.org
Call: (+44) 028 9047 2744
Write to: Youth Office, The Old Rectory, 217 Holywood Road,
           Belfast, BT4 2DH.

7. Church of Scotland
Contact: Steve Mallon (National Youth Advisor)
Visit: www.churchofscotland.org.uk/boards/
           parisheducation/peyouth
Email: enquiries@parish.ed.org.uk
Call: (+44) 08702 415748
Write to: Board of Education, Church of Scotland, 21 Young
           Street, Edinburgh, EH2 4HU.

8. Elim Churches
Contact: Mark Pugh (National Youth Coordinator)
Visit: www.Serious4God.co.uk
Email: mark@birminghamcc.co.uk
Call: (+44) 0121 236 2997
Write to: Serious4God, c/o Birmingham Christian Centre,
           Parade, Birmingham, B1 3QQ.

9. Methodist Church

Contact: Mike Seaton (National Youth Secretary)
Visit: www.mayc.info
Email: contact@mayc.info
Call: (+44) 020 7467 5209
Write to: MAYC, Methodist Church House, 25 Marylebone Road, London, NW1 5JR.

10. New Frontiers

Contact: Joel Virgo
Visit: www.newfrontiers.xtn.org
Email: admin@mobilise.fsnet.co.uk
Call: (+44) 01234 212620
Write to: New Frontiers Youth and Twenties, Woodside Christian Centre, Dover Crescent, Bedford, MK41 8QH.

11. New Testament Church of God

Contact: Dionne Gravesande
Visit: www.ntcg.org.uk
Call: (+44) 01604 643311
Write to: Youth and Christian Education Department, Main House, Overstone Park, Northampton, NN6 OAD.

12. Presbyterian Church in Ireland

Contact: Roz Stirling
Visit: www.pciyouth.org
Email: info@pciyouth.org
Call: (+44) 028 9032 2284
Write to: The Presbyterian Youth Office, Church House, Fisherwick Place, Belfast, BT1 6DW.

13. Roman Catholic Church

Contact: Helen Bardy (Youth Officer)
Email: cys@cbcew.org.uk
Call: (+44) 020 7834 1175
Write to: Catholic Youth Service, 39 Eccleston Square, London, SW1V 1BX.

14. Salvation Army

Contact: Russell Rook
Visit: www.youthministry.co.uk
Email: youth.ministries@salvationarmy.org.uk
Call: (+44) 020 8288 1202
Write to: Salvation Army Youth Ministries, 21 Crown Lane, Morden, Surrey, SM4 5BY.

15. United Reformed Church
Visit: www.furyonline.org.uk
Email: urc@urc.org.uk
Call: (+44) 020 7916 8647
Write to: FURY, The United Reformed Church, 86 Tavistock Place, London.

Christian Youth Organisations

1. Boys' Brigade
Description: A Christian youth organisation with over half a million members worldwide. The BB offers a wide range of activities, including games, crafts, sports, Christian teaching, music and holidays.
Visit: www.boys-brigade.org.uk
Email: feldon@boys-brigade.org.uk
Call: (+44) 01442 231681
Write to: Feldon Lodge, Hemel Hempstead, Hertfordshire, HP3 0BL.

2. Campaigners
Description: A Christian children's and youth movement, working in partnership with local churches across the UK. They provide training, resources and support for church-appointed leaders, enabling them to establish a relevant and holistic programme for all children and young people aged between 4 and 18.
Visit: www.campaigners.org.uk
Email: info@campaigners.org.uk
Call: (+44) 0870 8410757
Write to: Campaigner House, St Marks Close, Colney Heath, Nr St. Albans, Hertfordshire, AL4 0NQ.

3. Crusaders
Description: A dynamic interdenominational Christian youth organisation currently working with 19,000 children and young people across the UK.
Visit: www.crusaders.org.uk
Email: info@crusaders.org.uk
Call: (+44) 01582 589850
Write to: Crusaders, Smithfield House, Crescent Road, Luton, Bedfordshire, LU2 0AH.

4. CPAS (youth and children's ministry)

Description: Training, consultancy, resources and residential holidays (Ventures and Falcon Camps). Helping churches to serve children and young people effectively, helping them grow in faith as they grow in age, as well as helping churches to become all age communities in which people of every age are valued. Incorporating CYFA and Pathfinders.

Visit: www.cpas.org.uk

Email: mail@cpas.org.uk

Call: (+44) 01926 458458

Write to: CPAS, Athena Drive, Tachbrook Park, Warwick, CV34 6NG.

5. Frontier Youth Trust

Description: A Christian network dedicated to advancing the kingdom of God by supporting, resourcing and training those working with and on behalf of disadvantaged or marginalized young people.

Visit: www.fyt.org.uk

Email: frontier@fyt.org.uk

Call: (+44) 0121 687 3505

Write to: Unit 209f, The Big Peg, 120 Vyse Street, Birmingham, B18 6NF.

6. Girls' Brigade

Description: A Christian, international charity working alongside girls and young women of every background, ability and culture. Founded in 1893, it has become known as a fun, interesting, challenging and relevant provider of activities, skills, care and Christian love for hundreds of thousands of young people.

Visit: www.girlsbrigadeew.org.uk

Email: info@girlsbrigadeew.org.uk

Call: (+44) 01235 510425

Write to: Girls Brigade House, Foxhall Road, Didcot, Oxfordshire, OX11 7BQ.

7. Oasis Youth Action

Description: Demonstrating that Christian faith works by empowering young people and equipping volunteer and full-time youth workers.

Visit: www.oasistrust.org/youthaction

Email: youthaction@oasistrust.org

Call: (+44) 020 7450 9044

Write to: Oasis, 115 Southwark Bridge Road, London, SE1 0AX.

8. Youth for Christ

Description: Taking good news relevantly to every young
                person in Britain through mission teams, resources
                and training.
Visit: www.yfc.co.uk
Email: yfc@yfc.co.uk
Call: (+44) 0121 550 8055
Write to: YfC, PO Box 5254, Halesowen, West Midlands, B63
                3DG

9. Youth Link NI

Description: Provides training opportunities for young people
                and youth workers in all areas of Northern Ireland
                working with church, para-church and community
                based organisations.
Visit: www.youthlink.org.uk
Email: info@youthlink.org.uk
Call: (+44) 028 9032 3217
Write to: 143a University Street, Belfast, BT7 1HP.

Curriculum and resources

1. Alpha for Youth

Description: Youth version of the popular Alpha Course.
Visit: www.alphacourse.org
Email: info@alphacourse.org
Call: 0845 644 7544.

2. Cell Church UK

Description: Encourages and promotes the development of
                relevant cell churches across the denominations in
                the United Kingdom; provides a range of resources
                and training.
Visit: www.cellchurch.co.uk
Email: celluk@oval.com
Call: (+44) 01582 463232.

3. CYFA and Pathfinder Series

Description: Twenty resource books, each containing ten
                Bible-based teaching sessions for 14-18s, with a fur-
                ther six for 11-14s.
Visit: www.cpas.org.uk
Email: cyfa@cpas.org.uk
Call: (+44) 01926 458458

4. Damaris

Description: Damaris helps people develop a firm grasp of the Bible, a clear understanding of today's world, and the ability to connect one to the other.

Visit: www.damaris.org

Call: (+44) 02380 315319.

5. One Small Barking Dog

Description: Engages contemporary culture with creative communication fused with Christian spirituality. Provides creative video resources and images for use in multimedia worship events and youth groups.

Visit: www.osbd.org

Email: info@osbd.org

Call: (+44) 0121 683 6040

Write to: Studio 310, The Custard Factory, Gibb Street, Birmingham, B9 4AA.

6. Rock Solid

Description: Creative and energetic three year programme for 11-14 years olds produced by YfC.

Visit: www.yfc.co.uk

Email: rocksolid@yfc.co.uk

Call: (+44) 0121 550 8055.

7. Wesley Owen Direct

Description: Online Christian bookshop, stocking a diverse range of Christian books, resources, music and videos.

Visit: www.wesleyowen.com

8. Youth Specialties

Description: Provides quality resources, training, and encouragement for youth workers in churches and other youth-serving organisations throughout North America and the world. UK distribution of resources managed by YfC.

Visit: www.youthspecialties.com

9. Youthwork Magazine

Description: Monthly magazine for Christian youth workers, providing news, features, ready-to-use resources and recruitment opportunities.

Visit: www.youthwork.co.uk

Christian Youth Festivals and Holidays

1.   Christian Camping International

Description: An association of Christian centres, organisations and individuals involved in camps, holidays,
conference and outdoor activity ministries. Members
include over 115 Christian conference centres and
outdoor activity centres, 44 Christian holidays and
camps organisations, and over 60 individuals.

Visit: www.cci.org.uk
Email: office@cci.org.uk
Call: (+44) 01908 641641
Write to: CCI, 2 Leon House, Queensway, Bletchley, Milton
Keynes, Bedfordshire, MK2 2SS

2.   Cross Rhythms

Visit: www.crossrhythms.co.uk
Email: admin@crossrhythms.co.uk
Call: 08700 118008
Write to: Cross Rhythms, PO Box 1110, Stoke on Trent,
Staffordshire, ST1 1XR

3.   Cru Holidays

Visit: www.crusaders.org.uk
Email: tsmith@crusaders.org.uk
Call: (+44) 01582 589841
Write to: Cru Holidays, Smithfield House, Crescent Road,
Luton, Bedfordshire, LU2 OAH.

4.   CYFA Ventures and Falcon Camps

Visit: www.ventures-online.com
Email: ventures@cpas.org.uk
Call: (+44) 01926 458456

5.   Greenbelt

Visit: www.greenbelt.org.uk
Email: info@greenbelt.org.uk
Call: (+44) 020 7374 2755
Write to: Greenbelt Festivals, All Hallows on the Wall, 83
London Wall, London, EC2M 5ND

6.   Scripture Union

Visit: www.scriptureunion.org/holidays
Email: davidc@scriptureunion.org.uk
Call: (+44) 01908 856177
Write to: Scripture Union Holidays, 207-209 Queensway,
Bletchley, Milton Keynes, Buckinghamshire, MK2 2EB.

7. Soul Survivor

Visit: www.soulsurvivor.com
Email: info@soulsurvivor.com
Call: (+44) 0870 0543331
Write to: Soul Survivor, Unit 2, Paramount Industrial Estate, Sandown Road, Watford, Hertfordshire, WD24 7XF.

8. Spring Harvest

Visit: www.springharvest.org
Email: info@springharvest.org
Call: (+44) 01825 769111
Write to: 14 Horsted Square, Uckfield, East Sussex, TN22 1QG.

9. Summer Madness

Visit: www.summermadness.co.uk
Email: office@summermadness.co.uk
Call: (+44) 028 90 673379
Write to: Summer Madness, 217 Holywood Road, Belfast, BT4 2DH.

10. YfC Holidays

Visit: www.yfc.co.uk/church-resources/hols_details
Email: yfc@yfc.co.uk
Call: (+44) 0121 550 8055
Write to: YFC, PO Box 5254, Halesowen, West Midlands, B63 3DG.

Useful information

1. Adventure Activities Licensing Authority

Description: Licenses activity centres and other activity providers on behalf of the Department for Education and Skills (DfES), provides guidance for group organisers and a directory of licensed providers
Visit: www.aala.org
Email: enquiries@aala.org
Call: (+44) 029 2075 5715
Write to: 17 Lambourne Crescent, Cardiff Business Park, Llanishen, Cardiff, CF14 5GF.

2.   Amaze

Description: Association of Christian youth and children's
workers. Promoting safe practice, recruitment and
employment practice through the provision of advice
and resources.

Visit: www.amaze.org.uk
Email: admin@amaze.org.uk
Call: (+44) 0121 503 0824
Write to: PO Box 5254, Hinckley, LE10 2YX.

3.   Children and Young People's Unit

Description: Supporting government ministers to co-ordinate
policy-making across departments and removing
barriers enabling better coordination to happen effectively. Promoting active dialogue and partnership
with children, young people and with the voluntary
sector.

Visit: www.cypu.gov.uk
Email: mailbox@cypu.gsi.gov.uk
Call: 0870 000 2288
Write to: Children and Young People's Unit, Level 4E, Caxton
House, 6-11 Tothill Street, London, SW1H 9NA.

4.   Churches' Child Protection Advisory Service

Description: Child protection advice, training, resources and
access to Disclosure CRB checks for churches and
Christian organisations.

Visit: www.ccpas.co.uk
Email: enquiries@ccpas.co.uk
Call: 0845 120 4550
Write to: CCPAS, PO Box 133, Swanley, Kent BR8 7UQ.

5.   Churches' Agency for Safeguarding

Description: Provides free Criminal Records Bureau
Disclosure checks for congregations of denomina-
tional members.

Visit   www.churchsafe.org.uk
Email: david.dalziel@churchsafe.org.uk
Call: (+44) 020 7467 5216
Write to: Churches' Agency for Safeguarding, Methodist
Church House, 25 Marylebone Road, London NW1
5JR.

6. Community Transport Association

Description: Campaigns for minibus safety and provides
                driver training, information and resources for volun-
                tary and community transport organisations
Visit: www.communitytransport.com
Email: ctauk@communitytransport.com
Call: 0870 774 3586
Write to: Highbank, Halton Street, Hyde, Cheshire, SK14 2NY.

7. Department for Education and Skills

Visit: www.dfes.gov.uk/youngpeople/working
Email: info@dfes.gsi.gov.uk
Call: 0870 000 2288.

8. Evangelical Alliance Children's and Youth Network

Description: Networking and resourcing national and local
                youth organisations and workers; free monthly email
                bulletin; day conferences.
Visit: www.eauk.org/yac
Email: yac@eauk.org
Call: (+44) 0207 582 0228
Write to: Children's and Youth Network, Evangelical Alliance,
                Whitefield House, 186 Kennington Park Road,
                London, SE11 4BT.

9. National Youth Agency

Description: Promoting young people's personal and social
                development, and their voice, influence and place in
                society. Funded primarily by the Local Government
                Association and government departments, it works to
                improve and extend youth services and youth work,
                enhance and demonstrate youth participation in soci-
                ety, and promote effective youth policy and provision.
Visit: www.nya.org.uk
Email: nya@nya.org.uk
Call: (+44) 0116 285 3700
Write to: 17-23 Albion Street, Leicester, Leicestershire, LE1 6GD

10. Young People Now

Description: Weekly magazine for youth and community workers.
                Published in partnership with the National Youth Agency.
Visit: www.ypnmagazine.com
Email: ypn.editorial@haynet.com
Call: (+44) 020 8606 7500
Write to: Haymarket Professional Publications Ltd., 174
                Hammersmith Road, London, W6 7JP.

11. YouthInformation.com

Description: Youthinformation.com includes over 1000 information topics and holds contact details for more than
1200 national organisations, including hundreds of
built-in web links.
Visit: www.youthinformation.com
Email: youthinformation@nya.org.uk

12. Youthwork Magazine

Description: Monthly magazine for Christian youth workers,
providing news, features, ready-to-use resources and
recruitment opportunities.
Visit: www.youthwork.co.uk
Email: youthwork@premier.org.uk
Call: (+44) 01892 652364
Write to: Youthwork Magazine, CCP Limited, Broadway
House, The Broadway, Crowborough, TN6 1HQ

Telephone help Lines

1.   Childline

Description: ChildLine is the free, 24-hour helpline for children and young people in the UK to call about any
problem, at any time – day or night
Visit: www.childline.org.uk
Call: 0800 1111

2.   Churches' Child Protection Advisory Service

Description: 24 hour help line for churches and Christian
organisations providing child protection advice.
Visit: www.ccpas.co.uk
Call: 0845 120 4551

3.   Citizens Advice Bureau

Description: Provides up-to-date, independent advice, around
the clock and covers advice for England, Northern
Ireland, Scotland and Wales
Visit: wwww.adviceguide.org

4.   Connexions Direct

Description: Information and advice for those aged 13 to 19
years on issues relating to health, housing, relationships with family and friends, career and learning
options, money, and activities you can get involved in.
Visit: www.connexions-direct.com
Call: 080 800 13-2-19

5. **National Aids Helpline**
    Call: 0800 567123

6. **National Drugs Helpline**
    Description: Gives information and advice to anyone in the
                 UK concerned about drugs. This includes drug users,
                 their families, friends and people who work with
                 them.
    Visit: www.talktofrank.com
    Call: 0800 77 66 00

7. **Samaritans**
    Description: Samaritans provides confidential emotional sup-
                 port, 24 hours a day for people who are experiencing
                 feelings of distress or despair, including those which
                 may lead to suicide. You don't have to be suicidal to
                 call us. We are here for you if you're worried about
                 something, feel upset or confused, or you just want
                 to talk to someone.
    Visit: www.samaritans.org
    Call: 08457 90 90 90

8. **Shelter**
    Description: Shelterline is Britain's first 24-hour, free, national
                 housing help line. It provides advice to anyone with
                 a housing problem. Whatever time you need it; wher-
                 ever you are in Britain.
    Visit: www.shelter.org.uk
    Call: 0808 800 4444

9. **Victim Support**
    Description: A national charity which helps people affected by
                 crime. It provides free and confidential support.
    Visit: www.victimsupport.org.uk
    Call: 0845 30 30 30

Youthwork – the Partnership

Oasis, the Salvation Army, Spring Harvest, Youth for Christ and Youthwork Magazine are working together to equip and resource the church for effective youth work and ministry.

Youthwork – the Initiatives

1. *Youthwork – the Conference*
- An annual training conference to inspire, network and equip – managed by Spring Harvest. www.youthworkconference.co.uk

2. *Youthwork – the Magazine*
- A monthly magazine providing ideas, resources and guidance – managed by CCP. www.youthwork.co.uk

3. *Youthwork – the Training*
a) What Every Volunteer Youth Worker Should Know
- A nine-session/18-hour foundation course for volunteer youth workers – managed by Oasis Youth Action, with support from the Salvation Army.
www.oasistrust.org/youthworkcourse

b) The Art of Connecting
- An eight-session/12-hour course for young people in 'three story' evangelism – managed by YfC.
www.yfc.co.uk

4. *Youthwork – the Website*
- A gateway to online resources, community, information and learning – managed by *Youthwork Magazine*.
www.youthwork.co.uk

5. *Youthwork – the Resources*
- A range of books and materials edited by Danny Brierley and John Buckeridge – managed by Spring Harvest Publishing, an imprint of Authentic Media.
    - Going Deeper – theory, theology and practice.
    - Developing Practice – 'how to' guides, methods and inspiration.
    - Resourcing Ministry – ready-to-use ideas.

Youthwork – the Partners

Oasis Youth Action

Oasis Youth Action, the youth division of Oasis Trust, empowers young people and equips youth workers.

Oasis Youth Participation empowers those aged 11 to 25 years
- *Passion* mobilises young people in social action.
- *Frontline Teams* is a UK-based gap year programme.
- *Global Action Teams* place young adults in different countries.

Oasis Youth Work Training equips youth workers and ministers
- *What Every Volunteer Youth Worker Should Know* is a 9 session/ 18 hour course for volunteers.
- *Youth Work Degree* (BA Hons/ DipHE) is a professional training programme in youth work and ministry.

Oasis Youth Esteem enables youth workers and church volunteers to support young people's personal, social and health education in their local schools.

Oasis Youth Inclusion tackles social exclusion among young people and children. It offers mentoring, group work and sexual health/relationship education.

To find out more about Oasis Youth Action:
Visit: www.oasistrust.org/youthaction
Email: youthaction@oasistrust.org
Phone: (+44) 020 7450 9044.
Write to: Oasis Youth Action, 115 Southwark Bridge Road, London, SE1 0AX, England.

Salvation Army Youth Ministry Unit

The Youth Ministry Unit exists to resource and develop youth work in 1000 Salvation Army centres around the UK and the Republic of Ireland. It works with the Salvation Army's 18 divisional headquarters to implement local strategies for corps/churches, church plants, youth congregations, social centres and youth inclusion projects. In creating leadership development and mission training programmes for young people, young adults and youth workers, the unit is constantly engaged in developing leaders and missionaries for a 21st century church. In pioneering new projects and programmes, the unit is committed to developing new models of mission. In prioritising the marginalised and the excluded, the unit aims to extend The Salvation Army's rich heritage of social action and social justice. It provides young people with regular opportunities to experience, and engage in, evangelism, worship, discipleship and social action within youth culture. At present the unit is developing a new sub-brand of The Salvation Army focused on young people and young adults. In all this the unit aims to equip, empower and enable young people to reinvent The Salvation Army in their own community, context and culture.

To find out more about the Salvation Army Youth Ministry Unit:

Visit: www.salvationarmy.org.uk
Email: youth@salvationarmy.org.uk
Phone: (+44) 020 8288 1202
Write to: Salvation Army Youth Ministry Unit, 21 Crown Lane, Morden, Surrey, SM4 5BY, England.

Spring Harvest

Spring Harvest is an inter-denominational Christian organisation whose vision is to "equip the Church for action". Through a range of events, conferences, courses and resources they seek to enable Christians to impact their local communities and the wider world. Spring Harvest Holidays provide an opportunity in France for relaxation and refreshment of body, mind and spirit.

Their Main Event, held every Easter, attracts some 60,000 Christians of all ages, of which over 10,000 are young people. This event also includes specific streams which cater for over 2000 students. Alongside the teaching programme, Spring Harvest provide a range of resources for young people and those that work in youth ministry.

To find out more about Spring Harvest:
Visit: www.springharvest.org
Email: info@springharvest.org
Phone: (+44) 01825 769000
Write to: Spring Harvest, 14 Horsted Square, Uckfield, East Sussex, TN22 1QG, England.

YfC

YfC, one of the most dynamic Christian organisations, are taking good news relevantly to every young person in Britain. They help tackle the big issues facing young people today. They're going out on the streets, into schools and communities and have changed the lives of countless people throughout the UK.

Their staff, trainees and volunteers currently reach over 50,000 young people each week and have over 50 centres in locations throughout the UK. They also provide creative arts and sports mission teams, a network of registered groups and a strong emphasis on '3 story' evangelism. YfC International works in 120 nations.

To find out more about YfC:
Visit: www.yfc.co.uk
Email: yfc@yfc.co.uk
Phone: (+44) 0121 550 8055
Write to: YFC, PO Box 5254, Halesowen, West
             Midlands B63 3DG, England.

Youthwork Magazine

Youthwork Magazine is published monthly by CCP Limited. It is Britain's most-widely read magazine resource for equipping and informing Christian youth workers. It provides ideas, resources and guidance for youth ministry. CCP also publish *Christianity+Renewal*, *Christian Marketplace* and *Enough* magazines. CCP is part of the Premier Media Group.

To find out more about Youthwork Magazine:
Visit: www.youthwork.co.uk
Email: youthwork@premier.org.uk
Phone: (+44) 01892 652364
Write to: Youthwork Magazine, CCP Limited,
               Broadway House, The Broadway,
               Crowborough, TN6 1HQ, England.

What others have said about this book:

The book contains plenty of 'nuggets' to encourage and equip voluntary youth workers in their on-going relationships with young people.

Yvonne Criddle, Church of England

Reading this book will enable 'extra-time' youth workers to know what they are doing and why.

Nick Lear, Baptist Union of Great Britain

If we are to see this generation of young people discovering, and living out, God's great plan for their lives then we need masses of volunteer leaders who are equipped for the task. This book is a vital resource for every volunteer youth leader!

Matt Summerfield, Crusaders

If you can't find what you need in this book you will find out where to get it! This book blends good practice, ministry tips and the tools needed to be a great youth leader. A must read, a lasting resource.

Richard Bromley, Youth for Christ

Danny is intelligent, compassionate, insightful and a youth work veteran. He writes as he lives.

Simon Jarvis, Assemblies of God/Youth Alive

This is a helpful and practical guide to some of the fundamentals of youth work for busy 'extra-timers' (volunteer youth workers). It's a readable, honest and often humorous book, based on Danny's own experience of working with both individuals and groups – enabling young people to grow as disciples of Jesus.

Geoff Harley-Mason, CPAS

Volunteers strapped for time and resources will find this an invaluable and accessible guide to both the theoretical and practical aspects of their work with young people.

Claire Lea, Amaze

The only way we can truly value those who choose to work with young people in a voluntary capacity is to help them understand what it is that they're being asked to do. With this book Danny Brierley has produced a resource that does exactly what it says on the cover. It will be a must-read for a generation of youth workers who have 'ended up' working with a youth group and who are unsure about what it is they are supposed to be doing.

Steve Mallon, Church of Scotland

With practical advice, illustrations from first-hand experience and a comprehensive resource directory, this book will be of huge benefit to the thousands of men and women in churches across the UK who volunteer their time to work with young people. I thoroughly recommend it.

Jim Partridge, Spring Harvest

A thorough, practical, insightful and indispensable tool in the hands of volunteer youth workers. This book should be kept within easy reach at all times.

Mark Pugh, Elim Pentecostal Church Movement

Youth workers will find this book a very welcome addition to their resources. It will give them a great deal to think about, and provide them with some practical solutions.

Pam Richards, Church in Wales

This is a book that will inspire you to dream dreams, but to ground these in reality at the same time. If I'd had this book when I started out, I would have avoided some of the mistakes I made as I fumbled along.

Gary Smith, Baptist Union of Scotland